Heracles and Athenian Propaganda

Also available from Bloomsbury

Chaos, Cosmos and Creation in Early Greek Theogonies: An Ontological Exploration, Olaf Almqvist
The Study of Greek and Roman Religions: Insularity and Assimilation, Nickolas P. Roubekas
The Violent Hero: Heracles in the Greek Imagination, Katherine Lu Hsu

Heracles and Athenian Propaganda

Politics, Imagery and Drama

Sofia Frade

BLOOMSBURY ACADEMIC
LONDON • NEW YORK • OXFORD • NEW DELHI • SYDNEY

BLOOMSBURY ACADEMIC
Bloomsbury Publishing Plc
50 Bedford Square, London, WC1B 3DP, UK
1385 Broadway, New York, NY 10018, USA
29 Earlsfort Terrace, Dublin 2, Ireland

BLOOMSBURY, BLOOMSBURY ACADEMIC and the Diana logo are trademarks of Bloomsbury Publishing Plc

First published in Great Britain 2023
Paperback edition published 2025

Copyright © Sofia Frade, 2023

Sofia Frade has asserted her right under the Copyright, Designs and Patents Act, 1988, to be identified as Author of this work.

Cover image: Detail of *Heracles and the Centaur* by Giambologna 1529–1608
Photograph by Ken Wiedemann/Getty

All rights reserved. No part of this publication may be reproduced or transmitted in any form or by any means, electronic or mechanical, including photocopying, recording, or any information storage or retrieval system, without prior permission in writing from the publishers.

Bloomsbury Publishing Plc does not have any control over, or responsibility for, any third-party websites referred to or in this book. All internet addresses given in this book were correct at the time of going to press. The author and publisher regret any inconvenience caused if addresses have changed or sites have ceased to exist, but can accept no responsibility for any such changes.

A catalogue record for this book is available from the British Library.

A catalog record for this book is available from the Library of Congress.

ISBN:	HB:	978-1-4725-0559-0
	PB:	978-1-3503-7067-8
	ePDF:	978-1-4725-1115-7
	eBook:	978-1-4725-1043-3

Typeset by RefineCatch Limited, Bungay, Suffolk

To find out more about our authors and books visit www.bloomsbury.com and sign up for our newsletters.

ὅστις δὲ πλοῦτον ἢ σθένος μᾶλλον φίλων

ἀγαθῶν πεπᾶσθαι βούλεται, κακῶς φρονεῖ.
Eur., Herc. 1425–6

To my very good friends

Contents

1 Introduction 1
2 Propaganda and Politics in Athens 13
3 Transforming The Hero: Heracles and Athenian Ideology 41
4 Forsaking the Tripod: Heracles in Athenian Architecture 61
5 Crossing Boundaries: What Is It to Be a Hero? 81
6 Into Athens: Old Gods and New Gods 99
7 Conclusion 123

Notes 129
Bibliography 147
Index 161

1

Introduction

ἄρξομαι δὲ ἀπὸ τῶν προγόνων πρῶτον

(we shall begin with those who were born before us)

Pericles at Thuc. 2.36.1

Imagine yourself seated at the Theatre of Dionysus at Athens under the spring sun. Forget about the tourists with their cameras. Imagine the late fifth century BC. The theatre as you know it is not really there yet, just benches built on the hill. You have just participated in the purification rituals, the pouring of libations by ten Athenian generals, the public award of golden crowns, the yearly tribute of Athenian allies being displayed in the theatre, the parade of the war orphans. Now the herald announces the performances that will be presented in the following days. This year, Euripides will present in his trilogy a tragedy called *Heracles*. What thoughts cross your mind?

The answer to that question depends on who you are and what you know about Greek tragedy, Euripides, Heracles and even ancient Athens in general. Possibly you know absolutely nothing about these things and you are simply amazed at the display of bright colours on buildings you had always thought to be white. Maybe you know enough to realize you are at the Great Dionysia. Perhaps you know so much that you think of all the adaptations through the centuries inspired by this play: from Seneca to twenty-first-century CE stage adaptations, even Disney.

But imagine for a minute that you were born in the fifth century, imagine you were born in Greece. The colours of the Parthenon would come as no shock to you, nor would all the rituals: after all, you have participated in them, year after year. You know nothing of the 'modern' reception of the play, you do not even know what part of the Heracles myth Euripides' play is really about.

What thoughts then cross your mind? Of course, the answer to this question would be different from person to person: are you a sophist? Or perhaps an Athenian farmer visiting the city during the Festivals? Or maybe you are an ambassador from an allied city coming to bring some of the tributes on display?[1] The hypotheses are endless and a single straight answer is obviously impossible to give. Ultimately every person in the theatre that day would have had different thoughts on the play just announced.

These questions, of course, draw on a much larger subject: the interaction of tragedy with culture and politics. Heracles was not an unfamiliar figure to anyone in the audience. He was represented in the Agora, he had temples, he had a widespread cult in Attica, he was in most houses on all kinds of pottery, and he was in the stories told everywhere. Heracles was omnipresent. He had been used politically by Peisistratus as a representation of his power. His descendants formed the main politicized myth in Spartan ideology. All this was 'natural' knowledge shared by most people in the audience. None of these mental representations were left outside of the theatre on the day of the performance. There was a shared knowledge about the hero with which both the author and the audience could play. Reframing the play within that shared knowledge will certainly enrich the readings of this play and hopefully bring it back within a few shades of its original colours.

The assumption that *Heracles* is a strongly political play is not found except in the most recent bibliography. For example, in the late 1960s, Conacher (1967) does not list this play with the political plays (the *Supplices* and the *Heraclidae*) but with what he calls 'Mythological Tragedy', that is with the *Hippolytus* and the *Bacchae*. Neither did Zuntz in the 1950s situate this play in his *Political Plays*. I think, however, that most of the problems normally attributed to this play can be solved if we shift the focus in order to read it as a political play in the light of its political context.

Heracles is an alphabetic play: it does not belong to the canonical selection of Euripidean plays, and it has not been spared harsh criticism. Most studies in the nineteenth and twentieth centuries were centred on the question of the unity of the play.[2] The first of such studies was by Wilamowitz (1889) who criticized the play, namely its apparent lack of unity. The unity and structure of the play remained the focus of research for many decades after Wilamowitz's work,[3] with many defending the role of friendship and heroism as unifying.[4]

There have been a few studies that focus on some aspects of the play against the background of Athenian democracy, but mainly in terms of ritual and structures of citizenship.[5] Conacher follows this thread and argues that the innovations made in the plot do accentuate a certain humanism of the play: the fact that the labours and the subservience to Eurystheus are seen as a way to bring Amphitryon back to his native Mycenae, and the existence of Lycus, allow a representation of Heracles as a protector of his family. The movement to Athens, as opposed to Mt Oeta, also makes the audience focus on the humanization of the hero and the importance of human *philia*. This human *philia* is even more emphasized by the fact that the gods represented in the play seem to underline the gratuitousness with which Heracles was treated.[6] Thus, what Conacher describes as apparently juxtaposed action serves to underline the difference in behaviour between divine selfish actions and human generous friendship.

More recent approaches have departed from the traditional view of the play as twofold in order to find it tripartite.[7] Burnett, for example, also sees the play as a trilogy, where the first part shows Heracles saving his family, the second the destruction of his children and wife, and finally the third the redemption of the hero.[8]

Many have been the attempts to explain the apparent disorder and chaos of this play through the years.[9] I will argue in this book that many of these can be explained if we try to read the play illuminated by the role of Heracles in Athenian ideology, namely, the aristocratic and Panhellenic hero that poses a threat until he is integrated in the Athenian polis. I would also like to suggest that much of the apparent lack of unity and contrary movements in the play are there to stress the chaos and disorder of the old heroic and aristocratic world: a world where supplicants are not respected, where gods act somehow incomprehensibly and where individuals are a menace to the group. This world is contrasted with the redemption offered by Athens in the third part of the play.

My book relies heavily on the articulation of text and material culture. One of the reasons why literature and material culture are not usually put together is that presented by Taplin in *Pots and Plays*:

> **Last, and not least, experts have been** traditionally trained as either scholars of language and literature (in some contexts known as 'philologists') or

scholars of material culture (usually called 'archaeologists'). It may seem universally agreed that interdisciplinary explorations are highly desirable but in practice the professionals have tended to remain territorial and partisan.

2007: 3, original emphasis

Interdisciplinarity does pose a serious challenge, not least because of the education and formation of the researchers. The other main challenge is the way in which the articulation between tragedy and politics has been studied. Goldhill notes three main ways in which this relationship has been studied: one is to 'locate a narrowly and specific political message in a play', an example is the reading of Sophocles' *Oedipus Tyrannus* as a play on Pericles; the second is to understand how tragedy 'contributes to the understanding of the political process itself'; and the last one, connected with the previous is to study the 'deployment of mythic narrative' mainly to understand the ways in which myth and rituals inform 'a sense of political order fundamental to the citizens as political subjects'.[10]

The approach in this book underlines the existence of certain common background knowledge for any given society, an ideology that is always present and that informs the reading of a certain text. In this context, intertextuality is fundamental to fully understand the cultural background. Intertextuality reinforces the role of previous literary texts to shape possible meanings and readings. With this approach, from the mid-1960s, the relationship between texts is underlined. In the field of ancient literature, Lyne's *Further Voices* is without doubt a landmark, as the author states: 'to read the *Aeneid* is to be constantly aware of other texts in and behind the new creation' (1987: 103).

This intertextuality, however, is not restricted to texts: all means of communication can be used to create an ideology and to inform certain readings. The context of reception is always fundamental, as a 'transsubjective horizon of understanding conditions' always influences the reception (Jauss 1982: 3).

The question of the intemporality of the text was radically challenged by Jauss' theory of reception (Jauss and Bahti 1982). Even if his literary theory has been seriously challenged, the fact remains that the idea that a text can be freed from its original context and brought to a contemporary one, that a text is not necessarily 'monological',[11] is fundamental in the case of Greek tragedy and the understanding of its history of reception and performance. On top of that, the fact that fifth-century tragedy was a performative genre and despite any written versions of the text, the performance was always the most widespread and relevant form, gives the idea of context a particularly strong importance to this genre.

The importance of a certain context to understand a certain reading is still relevant in contemporary readings. In the 1980s, New Historicism was the culmination of this process, relating text with context and power. 'New Historicists consider literature as being just one among a multitude of social discourses that all participate in establishing and interpreting a common view of the world and human society.'[12] But there is a problem with this approach: 'since new historicism is, from the outset, interested in the social effects of literary production, it follows logically that it will pay more attention to these collective phenomena than to individual texts'.[13]

The location of the text in a certain material context was not facilitated by a general tendency as illustrated by archaeology that tended to look at the buildings, or even parts of the buildings, independently and not in dialogue with the space around them.[14] However, in the last years, new approaches are being proposed that change this methodology.

For example, Scott identifies three levels of resolution for the study of space: the micro-level, the macro-level and the semi-micro level: the micro and macro, i.e. the focus on particular landscapes or wider buildings, has been quite prolific in scholarship:

> Scholars have looked at how the individual structures use the space (a synchronic and often isolated space) but they have not looked at how the changing space, and what it contains, influences the particular structures.
>
> 2010: 20

This approach is not completely new but follows Clarke who claims that: 'it has slowly emerged that there is archaeological information in the spatial *relationships* between things as well as in the *things* in themselves' (1977: 5). These relationships are situated in what Scott calls the 'middle level', an approach that uses both the context and the information given by micro- and macro-methodologies. This way of approach also allows us to understand that the significance of something is not static, it varies according to who is perceiving it, as Scott states: 'A Spartan warrior, for example, coming to Athens would not have understood the polis in the same way as an Athenian philosopher' (2010: 21–3).

More recently, Neer and Kurke have suggested a new approach that proposes a methodology to read archaeology in the way that lyric is normally read: 'different. In place of thematics and iconography, the present study emphasizes syntagmatic relations, both intra- and extratextual.'[15] This methodology involves three components:

> The resulting lyric archaeology has three components. First, an ecumenical approach to evidence, in which multiple archives (literary, epigraphic, archaeological, art-historical) coexist. Second, an emphasis on close reading as a response to the complexity of the evidence and the questions of meaning and value that animate it. Third, an emphasis on grammars of concepts and rules of combination: the material, even *political* conditions of possibility for spatial involvement.[16]

The methodology of this book is somewhat similar to the approach purposed by Neer and Kurke. In Chapters 3 and 4, I will look into a wide range of evidence to inform the multiple ways in which Heracles could have been understood in fifth-century Athens. Then, in Chapters 5 and 6, I will procced to a close reading of the play about Heracles built on the information gathered in the first chapters. However, more than questions of spatiality, the focus of my research will be on how these readings are articulated with Athenian ideology and how they can procced from it, and reinforce it.

Fundamental to my readings, however, is the question of performance. Since the publication of Taplin's *The Stagecraft of Aeschylus* in 1977, there has been an increased interest in tragedy as performance, substantiated by the growing research on modern and contemporary reception of classical drama. This approach brought to light new concepts and methodologies, for example Fischer-Lichte in 2009 and 2010[17] underlined the importance of the co-presence in performance of both the performers and the audience and has defended that meaning in a performance is co-created by all participants, including the audience.

Thompson has defined performance as 'a surface in which the capacities for habitual interrogation and ethical dialogue take place in a tension of personalized decipherment' (2003: 150–1). This definition highlights two relevant concepts: the idea of surface and the idea of tension. I would like to propose an approach based on these concepts.

Tragedy is always performed in a series of tensions including the tension between individual and collective beliefs and readings. Individual readings of original performances of tragedy are mainly lost to us. It is, however, possible to try to understand how the performance of a play would have interacted with commonly held ideas and beliefs. Borrowing the concept of 'cultural code' from Barthes[18] and the idea of surface from Thompson, I would like to entertain the idea of a 'cultural surface' as the cultural manifestations of a specific group. This idea of 'cultural surface' does not imply uniformity, on the contrary, it encompasses both collective-held beliefs and the tension created by divergent individual beliefs.

This idea of a cultural surface is, I suggest, important to reframe the idea of propaganda that will be discussed in the next chapter. One problem for the discussion of tragedy and propaganda is the way the term was influenced by twentieth-century uses of propaganda. This historical context has culturally changed the notion of propaganda as an evil thing that takes away the rational capacities of a people in order to make them support the most terrifying purposes. If, however, instead of a top-down approach, we see propaganda as part of this cultural surface, it is possible to understand better how cultural manifestations interact with those beliefs, while creating tensions and questioning them as well as serving as reinforcement. To give one example on how this cultural surface can interact and be a part of propaganda, I would like to refer to Boardman's statement on the political meaning of Attic vases:

> So did Athens' leaders use the potters' quarter as a tool of political propaganda? Of course not. The vase painters simply depicted scenes which found a response in their public because they were of stories which poets, priests and politicians had used to glorify and justify civic events and successes, in the usual Greek manner, using or inventing myth to suit each occasion.
>
> 2001: 208

The concept of cultural surface, of which propaganda can be a strand, could help us understand the communication dynamics implied in this situation: the reproduction of a certain iconography, instead of a straight top-down form of propaganda, can act as a sign that the political meaning associated with the image has been integrated into the cultural narrative of the audience.

As Griffin and Carter (2011) fully demonstrate, Attic tragedy can be many conflicting things at the same time. Of these contradictions, two are particularly relevant for my analysis of political readings: 'the meaning of each tragedy is both coherent and intelligible and multilayered and complex' and 'tragedies provided an individual stimulus for each audience member and had a collective psycho-social-behavioural impact on the audience' (pp. 2–3). Also, Barbato (2020) relates the construction of Athenian identity with the 'social memory of Athens' mythical past' (p. ix), this social memory is at play whenever mythical subjects are discussed, as within tragedy. Therefore, the author states:

> Athenian democratic ideology was a fluid set of ideas, values and beliefs shared by the Athenians as a result of a constant ideological practice influenced by the institutions of democracy. This process entailed the active participation of both mass and elite, and enabled the Athenians to produce multiple and compatible ideas about their community and its mythical past.[19]

This 'ideological practice' constitutes a vital part of the formation and maintenance of the cultural surface, and tragedy is a part of this process: by presenting nuanced narratives and bringing forth a space to hold, create and discuss complex ideas.

It is of the utmost importance to be able to hold contradictions and be aware of deep complexities when studying tragedy. Rather than a simplistic and all-encompassing reading of the play, my aim is to add another layer of nuance to the already existing readings, and, whenever possible, to make as clear as possible the ways in which the plays could have engaged with the original audience's cultural surface.

With Griffin and Carter, I mostly support the idea that the politics of tragedy are much more than a correlation between fiction and contemporary historical facts, but a complex dialogue with beliefs, ideologies and identities within the audience.[20] Kennedy highlights that tragedies are a part of an 'inherently connected system' and the playwrights were 'subject to this system as much or more than they shape it' (2009: 10). Yates, discussing the Greek memories of the Persian Wars and the construction of Greek identities also refers to 'shared memories in imagined communities do not emerge casually, as they might in a face-to-face community. Because of the distances involved, these memories must be propagated and then maintained through cultural devices' (2019: 13).

Naturally, these relationships spread to performances, rituals and discourse in general.[21] To add to all of these factors, I believe some preconceptions have detracted the attention of scholars from pursuing the exploration of such an ideological system on tragedy more deeply. First, as has been synthesized by Kennedy:

> The imperial implications behind tragedy have been largely left unmentioned, though now there is a growing literature in this direction. Because the general scholarly consensus recently has been that the empire was always oppressive, even when scholarship on tragedy does address it, the analysis almost always tends to view tragedy as critical of it. The *archê* was bad and tragedy is good; therefore tragedy must question empire.
>
> 2009: 4

All of these factors contribute to the lack of studies in Athenian propaganda and its relationship with drama. In a city so marked by iconographic propaganda, how did the imagery influence the audience? A few studies have been written which have posed this question. Three important examples are the readings of the *Ion* in the light of the architecture of the Acropolis, by Loraux (1990b), the *Trojan Women* by Kennedy (2009) and a more recent corpus of readings by Athanassaki.[22]

The present study tries to reconstruct the aspects of the Athenian cultural surface related to the figure of Heracles and shed new light on his role on stage. The main focus of this research is the Euripidean *Heracles*. The methodology of this research entails bringing the play back to its original context and trying to establish the potential relationships it would have had with its political and ideological context. More than to a literary context, the plays belonged to a civic, political, religious and ideological context.

My readings of the play strongly relate to previous research on the theme. Stafford (2012) and Ogden's *Handbook of Heracles* (2021), published while this book was under revision, offer a fundamental overview of the figure of Heracles in various moments and contexts. Papadopoulou (2005) and Griffiths (2006) offer readings of Euripides' play within the Athenian context. Many of my readings are similar and built upon their work. However, by focusing on the concept of propaganda, this book tries to identify patterns of usage of the hero across different media – myth, religion, civic iconography and tragedy – to support and promote Athenian ideology. This research led me to identify two roles in which Heracles was used to articulate Athenian ideology: on the one hand, a broader reading where Heracles represents the Panhellenic hero who is introduced to, initiated into and saved by Athens; on the other hand, Heracles can be seen as a model of integration of the aristocratic values within Athenian democracy. I believe that understanding the role of Heracles in Athenian propaganda in a broader context can help in understanding and clarifying Euripides' *Heracles*.

The book is organized into six chapters, followed by a short conclusion. The second chapter, after this introduction, reviews the literature on politics in religion and drama in ancient Athens and also discusses a working definition of propaganda and establishes the main strands of propaganda upon which the main argument of this book will be built: the idea of Athens as a place of salvation and their position in the Delian League, and the integration of the aristocracy in the new democratic model. Chapter 3 reviews the relationship of Heracles with Athens, with a particular focus on the shifts from Panhellenic myth to local variations. This chapter reviews evidence from pottery, religion and literature to argue that the figure of Heracles suffers a significant shift from violent to civilizational hero, which had a strong potential to be useful for Athenian politics and ideology. Chapter 4, while continuing the argument from the previous chapter, focuses on Athenian monumental architecture, where more than the cultural shift discussed before, I see the politically motivated interventions in the use of the Heracles' myth. These three chapters allow me to establish the role of Heracles within the Athenian cultural surface with a focus on the relation with ideology.

Finally, Chapters 5 and 6 analyse the intersection of ideology and cultural representation and the text of Euripides. By looking at the play within this framework, it is possible to see how the articulation with the cultural surface of the original audience brings to light new readings and helps make sense of some of the problems normally attributed to the play. Chapter 5 will consider the representation of Heracles as a hero and a model for Athenian aristocracy and Chapter 6 will review the complex theology of the play and argue that it aligns with the presentation of Athens (and Athena) as the space for salvation.

The Greek from *Heracles* follows the Oxford Classical Texts (OCT) by James Diggle (1981). Any other Greek quotations follow those available at the Loeb Library online as of the end of July 2021. The translations provided are my own: they are designed to help accompany the discussion and I tried to keep them to a bare minimum to maintain the text as fluent as possible.

This book is born out of my PhD thesis, therefore, my first thanks go to the institutions that made the PhD possible: the FCT for giving me a three-year fellowship, the School of Arts and Humanities of the University of Lisbon for allowing me to take a three-year leave, and the University of Oxford and the APGRD for having received me in the most welcoming way during those years.

I cannot thank Fiona Macintosh enough. I realize how rare it is to have had a supervisor with such generosity, availability and all-round support. This book would not exist without her encouragement. I have to thank Edith Hall for the first idea of this book and the liaison established with Bloomsbury Publishers over a gin on a Bastille Day, many years ago.

I extend my thanks to my Portuguese supervisors, Frederico Lourenço, who started this project with me, and José Pedro Serra, who took upon himself the task of accompanying my PhD to its conclusion.

I would also like to thank all the people who made themselves available to read and discuss particularly difficult parts of my thesis: Professor Robert Parker for his invaluable suggestions on Greek religion and for pointing out to me the importance of Eleusis for my argument; Professor Jeremy Waldron for his remarks on the politics of propaganda; Professor Oliver Taplin for his remarks on tragedy in general and *Ajax* in particular; and Professor Irene Lemos for reading and commenting on my chapter on archaeology.

My gratitude is also owed to my colleagues and friends who helped me in numerous ways: to Rodrigo Furtado for never letting me get comfortable with any kind of preconceived idea and for an infinite support; to Rui Pina Coelho for taking me out of my comfort zone in performance theory and for making me read Thompson's paper on Performance that ended up giving me a key concept for my argument; to Nelson Pinheiro who was fundamental in picking up bureaucratic tasks while I was at the final stages of writing this book and to Justine McConnell for always being available to go to the library and share the bits of bibliography I could not otherwise have set my eyes on, especially during a pandemic.

Finally, I would like to thank my students, who always make me rethink everything and keep me on my toes.

2

Propaganda and Politics in Athens

ἔπουδ' ἄμ' ἡμῖν πρὸς πόλισμα Παλλάδος.

(follow me to the city of Pallas)

Eur., *Herc.* 1323

Drawing on the idea of cultural surface stated in the previous chapter, this chapter has two main aims: to discuss the idea of propaganda in the context of Attic Tragedy and to establish the two main ideological tensions that will be further analysed in this book. In order to do that, the next two sections will start by providing a short framework of the questions surrounding the relationship of Attic tragedy and religion with politics.

The politics of tragedy

Drama fills the city with a democratic language, gives the wealthiest citizens the opportunity to show off their money, and brings all the community together in a relationship as a whole, as individuals, as citizens of Athens and as worshippers of the gods of the city. Tragedy is a phenomenon of the polis: the polis was everything, and everything was in the polis – the religion, the citizens, the justice, all institutions. But more than the polis, at least in the Great Dionysia, it is also a phenomenon of the empire, along with the citizens, the theatre would have been filled with foreigners and ambassadors of the Athenian allies. Hence, this was by far, one of the closest experiences to a modern 'mass media performance' of the time. Thus, we have performance financed by the city and by the wealthiest citizens, the plot of which is derived from some of the best used materials for propaganda: myth. We know that the Great Dionysia had important ideological moments: the ceremony in which the city awarded arms to the war orphans and the display of the tribute paid by the cities of the Delian League are two good examples.

These moments clearly make the stage of the Great Dionysia a perfect space to broadcast a certain image and ideology of the city. The relationship between the Great Dionisia and Athenian politics has been studied and argued by many scholars.[1] The rhetoric around Athenian ideology would be present not only in the performances but also in the public spaces and buildings.[2] How did the festivals and the building programme relate? On a first level, the festivals took place in a certain physical space, and the performances and rituals had assigned locations within the city. But more than that, both forms of rhetoric would have been used in order to propagate certain ideas.

Drama is directly related to the polis. Drama belongs to the polis, it has deep connections with it. It had various ways to engage the citizens. One was, of course, by being integrated in some of the major Attic Festivals. But it also appointed individual citizens. For example, Wilson claims that the institution of khoregia seeks to put private wealth at the service of the city, not only in relation to drama (1997: 96–7). It also stresses the importance of tragic khoregia as a particularly relevant leithourgia, namely due to the relative rarity of it: within Athens' festivals, there were many (about a hundred) chances to be a leithourgos, but only three to be a tragic choregos at the great Dionysia, moreover this role was not performed by a specific group within the Athenian society, it was available to any citizen who could afford it.[3]

Greek tragedy is in fact a particular kind of literature as it is composed having performance as the main outcome and has a highly political context. It is important to note that fifth-century Athenian culture was highly performative. It was not a strictly oral culture, since the written word was well known from the eighth century and some level of literacy would have been spread in the city, but the main medium of transmission was still oral.[4] Most people would know Homer, the lyric poets and drama not from a papyrus but from a performance. The normal citizen's life was wrapped in performances, as Simon Goldhill pointed out.[5]

Tragedy was not a written text read by an elite; it was a performance shown to a huge audience. And the context of the performance at the Great Dionysia was rather particular, as Pickard-Cambridge, Gould and Lewis point out, the importance of this festival was not only related to the great quality of the performances offered there, both dramatic and lyric, but due to the fact that it was open to anybody who wanted to attend it, being therefore 'an effective advertisement of the wealth and power and public spirit of Athens, no less than the artistic and literary leadership of her sons'.[6] The fact that the festival took place after the end of the winter and when it was possible to travel by sea again helped to reinforce this Panhellenic character, which was reinforced from the moment the allies at the Delian league swore to bring their tributes to Athens during the Great Dionysia.

It is important to stress that at the Great Dionysia, Athens was open to foreigners, many of them from the Athenian allies in the Delian League. Therefore, the festival was a very useful instrument in displaying the city's ideology. That the image of the city presented on stage was of major importance, even in comedy, is made clear by the famous passage of the *Acharnians* (502-4) where Aristophanes implies that it is not the same to criticize the city in the Lenaea when only citizens were present whereas in the Great Dionysia all sorts of visitors could be attending (οὐ γάρ με νῦν γε διαβαλεῖ Κλέων ὅτι | ξένων παρόντων τὴν πόλιν κακῶς λέγω | αὐτοὶ γάρ ἐσμεν οὑπὶ Ληναίῳ τ' ἀγών – Cleon cannot accuse me now of speaking badly about the city in the presence of strangers, since it is only us here at the Lenaea).

This passage also makes quite clear that the city would not approve the broadcasting of an image of itself very different from the official one; this does not mean that there was no room for discussion at the Great Dionysia, but the direct criticism of the city was not approved at the great imperial festival of the Athenians.

One of the very first studies to re-centre the performative aspects of tragedy was, of course, Taplin's *The stagecraft of Aeschylus*, which comes in a line started mainly by Webster[7] of relating literary and performative aspects. This area of research has attracted the works of some scholars like Green, Csapo and more recently Wilson and Taplin. All of these studies have been fundamental to our understanding of the close connection between material culture and drama and have highlighted the need for further work on these subjects. However, most of these studies are mainly concerned with the reception of tragedy in material culture, not so much on how material culture reinforced certain ideals and mentalities that were then used in the performances.

Since the 1980s, studies of tragedy and ideology became more and more important, with a series of studies that focus on the politics of tragedy and try to understand particular characters or plays within the ideology of the city. For example, Sophie Mills and Rebecca Futo-Kenedy focus on Theseus and Athena and try to understand how these characters represent the city or the idea of the city of Athens in different plays.[8] Tzanetou (2012) focuses on the importance of the topic of the suppliants and how its development goes along with the politics of the city.

Centuries of reception changed the focus of tragedy from Athenian politics to general questions of politics and humanity, the role of destiny, the gods, etc. This new approach was enforced when a selection of plays was made. A close look at titles of lost plays or at the alphabetical plays of Euripides shows that plays based on Athenian heroes like *Ion* and *Erechthonius* and plays on the Athenian role in the empire, like the *Supplices*, were left out of the canon and would have had a much bigger part in drama than we normally assume. A bit like the walls of the Acropolis, with time, the original colours faded and assumed the white, clean, look with which we now associate it. The centuries with all their history and very different contexts somehow stripped the Athenian culture of its more ethnic, unique values and turned it into a universal culture. Of course, this process is fundamental to the history of reception. However, we should not forget that there is that process mediating us from the original texts.

Polis religion and politics

The discussion of Greek religion and politics is a lengthy and heated one. It is not my aim to offer new data or give any original insight into the topic, but only to shed some light on what conclusions can be drawn from the relations between hero cults and politics, which will be relevant for our analysis of Heracles.

With her paper in 1990, Sourvinou-Inwood[9] defined the concept of polis religion and established a landmark for this discussion. For Sourvinou-Inwood, the idea of polis religion postulates that the polis provides the 'fundamental framework in which Greek religion operated', that is, the polis supplied the structure within which one was to perform and participate in the rituals. A major argument for this is that one was only to take part fully in the rituals of one's own polis. In the *sacred spaces* of other *poleis*, even in Panhellenic sanctuaries, one could only undergo rituals as a *xenos*, often with the mediation of a *proxenos*.

Religious authority was mainly under the control of the polis; priests and priestesses were appointed or selected by the city, and major decisions – even under oracular advice – were taken by the council.[10] In his liturgical duties, the priest acted as a symbolic mediator between men and the gods. It was the polis that placed him in that symbolic position, in the same way the polis decreed that magistrates could assume that role on certain occasions.

Priests are mainly seen as people appointed by the city so as to benefit the community (see, e.g., Plato, *Politicus* 290 c–d): the definition of a priest is someone who is skilled at appeasing the gods with sacrifices. This underlines a clear concept of Greek religion: gods need sacrifices and rituals in order to be beneficial, or at least, not be hazardous. These sacrifices and rituals, be they performed individually or by a community, must follow the gods' wishes. This is where the priests with their practical knowledge come into their own; they are 'ἐπιστήμονες'. Ultimately, however, the onus was on the individual or the community to make decisions about the cult.

At the same time, ritual would reinforce group solidarity by strengthening group bonds and defining it by contrast to other groups. One good example of this usage of ritual is the institution of the eponymous heroes' cult by Cleisthenes in order to reinforce the newly created division of Athenians by demes and tribes, giving each tribe a hero enabled the citizens to create an identity and community under their eponymous hero.

There have been many critics of this way of regarding Greek religion.[11] Many have criticized the fact that most of the polis religious discussion is centred on public rituals and disregards any private cult. But evidence about private practices is scant. It is worth noting that Plato (*Laws* 909d–910a) forbids private sacrifices and the establishment of private shrines. This means, first of all, that such practices did exist and was important to Greek religion, and also that for Plato, at least, religion derived its strength from its communal form and could be perverted if performed on personal terms. Any study on religion must acknowledge the fact that communal, polis-centred rituals were not the only rituals to be performed. An important portion of religious rituals performed were done so by individuals, families and clans.

Interestingly enough, one common example given to illustrate the importance of families and clans in religion is the case of the Alcmaeonidai building the Temple of Apollo at Delphi. Herodotus and Aristotle are the main sources (Hdt. 5. 62.3; Aristotle, *Ath. Pol.* 19.4), and they both highlight the fact that despite the plans to build the temple out of tufa, they made the front out of much more expensive Parian marble. And both authors relate this temple-building with the scheme plotted with the Spartans in order to overthrow the Peisistratids.

It is obvious that we have here a wealthy, powerful clan building a temple outside of their polis in a major Greek sanctuary. Herodotus' account even tells us that to show how wealthy they were, the temple was built out of Parian marble and not tufa as they had previously agreed.

Nevertheless, it is quite clear from both accounts that the temple was not built out of piety alone, but its construction also had clear political motivations. For, having been expelled from Athens by Hyppias, the Alcmaeonidai offered to build the new temple at Delphi so as to find political support for their anti-tyrant cause among the Spartans, a plan which eventually worked out for them. From this example it is not only evident that clans could play an important role in religion, separately from the polis, but also that that role could be performed with clear political intentions. The utility of great sanctuaries and important oracles in the development of politics is also made clear from this example.[12]

Nonetheless, the distinction between political and religious citizenship is not absolute. As Hansen and Nielson (2004: 131) underline, even if it is true that everyone belonged to the religious structure of his own polis, there is an important difference in politics that only men really belonged. At least in Athens, women were not *politai*. They did not take any part in political or military issues. They did, however, participate in rituals and festivals, playing sometimes a major role. No woman could be appointed as magistrate, but she could be elected as a priestess. This means that the view on who was fully enabled to participate in matters of the polis was not exactly the same as the view on who could participate in religion.

This concept of polis religion has been challenged by some authors that defend Greek religion as being far older than the concept of the polis itself, therefore Greek religion existed by itself without the framework of a polis. That does not mean that polis and religion are to be completely set apart, in fact, 'a predominant view is that the polis emerged out of the activities connected with the building of temples and the communal organization of religious festivals' (Hansen and Nielsen 2004: 132). Along with this line of thought go most of the criticisms made by Woolf (1997: 39 ff.) of the polis religion model: i.e. the fact that there was a civic authority regulating the religion of the polis does not explain most of the similar cults that coexisted at the same time, nor does it justify any innovation. Religion was not created by the poleis. It existed before and would go far beyond the collapse of the polis system.

Nevertheless, by the fifth century in Athens, religion and politics go hand in hand. Of course, no approach can be made without recognizing how little we know about Greek religious origins, personal religion and ritual. Even so, we have enough evidence to trace a clear connection between polis and religion, and the ways the city used ritual in order to support and define itself and to project a certain image.

Religion helps define identity. The Greeks viewed themselves as Greeks, not because of political affairs but, as Herodotus states, because they spoke the same language and worshipped the same gods (8.144.2).

Rituals were very important to group identity in two ways, by binding together the group and by differentiating them from other groups. Each polis would have specific rituals, patron gods, heroes and festivals that showed their identity and differentiated them from other *poleis*. One good example of this is the institution of the new tribes by Cleisthenes followed by the creation of rituals to honour the eponymous heroes performed by those tribes. As Ekroth states:

> Participating in the sacrifice to the hero and, most of all, in the consumption of the victim's meat clearly marked who belonged and who did not.
> 2009: 139

And heroes were particularly important to bond smaller groups together; by their nature they were easier to appropriate, their myths were more flexible and available to adapt to different necessities and contexts.

Good examples of this are the various episodes of bone transferrals.[13] The city that performed rituals to a hero would benefit from the protection of that hero, even if he had been an enemy of the city while alive or a protector of an antagonistic city. Herodotus gives us the account of the transferral of Orestes' bones to Sparta.[14] Around 560, the Spartans were unable to conquer Tegea. After consulting Delphi, they were told to acquire Orestes' bones and move them to Sparta. The bones were found at Tegea, brought to Sparta and finally the Spartans defeated the city.

Most of the bone-transferral episodes were clearly political and involved territorial disputes. Another important episode (though not directly linked with territorial claims because the bones were taken after military victory) is that of Theseus. After an oracle Cimon tries to obtain the hero's bones from Scyros but the inhabitants refuse to give them and are eventually subdued. As he comes back to Athens, it is as if the hero himself was returning, as described by Plutarch (*Theseus* 36.2).

The political implications are clear. Cimon had driven off the shadow of his father's (Miltiades) disgrace and tried to restore his family's great name in several ways.[15] The introduction of the Athenian major hero, Theseus, whose prominence in Attic art, myth and literature was growing thickly, was important political propaganda. McCauley underlines the importance of piety on such occasions; the cities involved in the transferral of the bones might have intended to follow the orders of Apollo, yet whatever religious and pious intentions these actions might have had, they certainly had very clear political consequences. These symbolic acts 'gave a political advantage to the cities which received the bones and in Theseus' case, to the person who seems to have engineered the removal. In the light of the important advantages gained by the movers, it seems probable that these acts were planned by the movers from the beginning.'[16]

The relationship between heroes, cult and politics is clearly at work here. And if it is true that heroes were far more plastic in order to fit a political agenda, sometimes gods were used in similar ways. A good example is the third return of Peisistratus to Athens. In his account, Herodotus tells us that the tyrant drove back to Athens in a chariot with Athena herself, as impersonated by a woman, guiding him. The goddess is the guardian of the city, and the returning tyrant is her *protégé* (Hdt. 1.60.3–5.). It is interesting, however, to see Herodotus' opinion on this scheme:

μηχανῶνται δὴ ἐπὶ τῇ κατόδῳ πρῆγμα εὐηθέστατον, ὡς ἐγὼ εὑρίσκω, μακρῷ, ἐπεί γε ἀπεκρίθη ἐκ παλαιτέρου τοῦ βαρβάρου ἔθνεος τὸ Ἑλληνικὸν ἐὸν καὶ δεξιώτερον καὶ εὐηθείης ἠλιθίου ἀπηλλαγμένον μᾶλλον, εἰ καὶ τότε γε οὗτοι ἐν Ἀθηναίοισι τοῖσι πρώτοισι λεγομένοισι εἶναι Ἑλλήνων σοφίην μηχανῶνται τοιάδε.

1.60.3

(They [Megacles and Peisistratus] contrived a plan for his return of the utmost silliness I ever found, seeing that the Greeks have, for a long time, been distinguished from the Barbarians for their dexterity and their lack of gullibility, if they really pull this trick with the Athenians, who are considered the wisest of the Greeks.)

We should not, though, follow blindly the account that the people of Athens were completely fooled by these events. The use of heroes and gods in political terms was not a one-sided plot: with a smart politician or family using the poor people's beliefs in order to deceive them. Myth was not a question of faith, it was not revealed truth. Myth was malleable, adaptable and the most important means of definition for individuals, families and cities. It is probable that people would have understood the way heroes and gods were being used, and thence were an active part in the construction of the narrative. It is also probable that Athenians knew perfectly well that that was not Athena, but somehow, they believed, or wanted to believe, that that man was actually a *protégé* of the goddess, that is, someone beneficial to their city, and eventually they were not completely wrong.

The choice of the language of myth over the language of history for political purposes is not a monologue but a dialogue, it is not something imposed by the elites, but co-created by the community. One of the best examples of this is the case of Harmodius and Aristogeiton.[17]

These are just a few examples of the way politics and religion worked together.[18] What I think cannot be denied, after we look closely at a few examples, is that religion was indeed used in political terms. Or better yet, worked together with in order to provide a certain image of the polis, in order to unite the citizens, in order to create new categories among them, as in the case of the eponymous heroes, in order to establish and keep power over other cities, in order to justify alliances.

It is important to clarify when we talk about polis religion that the evidence we have access to is probably only a minute fraction of all the evidence. Each new inscription can shine new light on religious matters, and for this reason no conclusions can be regarded as final or universal. It is also important to understand that regarding the usage of cults or cultic figures to achieve certain political objectives was not a deceptive way of manipulating general opinion. As we can see clearly in the case of Harmodius and Aristogeiton (and as we may suspect in the Athena-Peisistratus scene) it was more than a plot presented to a passive audience unable to recognize an alternative version or an impersonation. It was a game played by both sides and with benefits to both sides. The Athenians were not deceived in believing that Athena was physically there or Hipparchus was the tyrant and democracy started right after his death. They were given a version of the facts and they accepted it. And, I would argue, they did so willingly.[19] This case demonstrates a willingness to co-create a narrative that best suits the ideological purposes of the city.

Propaganda in ancient Athens

In order to define the term 'propaganda' and to discuss whether it can be applied to fifth-century Athens, this section will present a short overview of the usage of this term so as to achieve a working definition. The application of the term to classical antiquity in general and Athenian democracy in particular is neither widespread nor uncontroversial. The term propaganda does not exist in the ancient world. The first use of the word with the meaning we give it today dates back to the seventeenth century with the creation, by the Catholic Church, of the *Congregatio De Propaganda Fide* in the context of the Counter-Reformation.

The concept, of course, was widespread during the Second World War and Cold War, which gave it its darkest overtones. Consequently, most of the studies on propaganda focus on the twentieth-century phenomena. The term, however, is fairly frequently used in Classical Studies, but most of the time without a theoretical framework or a clear definition. One of the few examples of an attempt to make a systematic study of ancient propaganda is by the group directed by Marta Sordi at the Catholic University of Milan in the

1970s.[20] A rare example of a case study following the methodology for modern propaganda studies is the article on Ion and Kresphontes by Bremmer (1997).[21]

Even if it is true, however, that the term propaganda is quite frequently applied to the ancient world, there is considerable dissent. For example, Zanker, in his classic book on the power of images in Augustan's politics, without further development on the question of propaganda, simply states:

> the goal of this book is to examine the complex interrelationship of the establishment of monarchy, the transformation of society, and the creation of a whole new method of visual communication. Recent experience has tempted us to see in this a propaganda machine at work, but in Rome there was no such thing.
>
> 1990: 3

In order to discuss the existence of propaganda in the Greek world, it is important to clarify concepts. In the literature the definitions vary enormously. Hornblower states that propaganda involves 'active manipulation of opinion and some distortion of the truth'.[22] Lasswell gives a broad definition when he states that propaganda is 'the technique of influencing human action by the manipulation of representations. These representations may take spoken, written, pictorial or musical form'.[23] Both definitions focus on the idea of manipulation of information and representations.

Recent propaganda analysis tends to focus on the role of the propagandist; thus, Jowett and O'Donnell offer the following definition:

> Propaganda is the deliberate, systematic attempt to shape perceptions, manipulate cognitions, and direct behavior to achieve a response that furthers the desired intent of the propagandist.
>
> 2006: 7

Following Ellul's (1973) approach to propaganda, Evans focuses on its educational aspect:

> I may define propaganda as the educational efforts or information used by an organized group that is made available to a selected audience, for the specific purpose of making the audience take a particular course of action or conform to a certain attitude desired by the organized group.
>
> 1992: 1

One of the biggest problems in defining propaganda is that, if taken too broadly, the definitions would be similar to those of 'persuasion' or even 'communication'; and if taken too strictly, the definition would not be able to incorporate all forms of propaganda present in the modern world.

In his book *Propaganda*, Ellul refuses to define the term, instead he offers a few characteristics that should be present in modern propaganda.[24] Propaganda, according to Ellul, should be addressed at once to the individual and to the masses; it must be total in the sense that it makes use of all the media available; it should be continuous and lasting; it must have a centralized organization and it should lead the masses to a certain orthopraxy.

Ellul also gives four groups of binary factors that should cover all kinds of propaganda. Propaganda should be: political or sociological, of agitation or integration, horizontal or vertical, rational or irrational. Political propaganda corresponds to the main definition of propaganda. On the other hand, sociological propaganda is the set of mechanisms used by a group to express itself and its identity that serves both to bind the group together and to define itself against other groups on which they might want to impose their ideology.[25]

Propaganda of agitation is mainly opposition propaganda as propaganda of integration aims to reinforce the sense of belonging to a community and support the already ongoing policies. Even though Ellul only operates with this kind of model for the contemporary world (1973: 74), Evans (1992) applies this concept to ancient Rome which opens the possibility of applying it to the ancient world. Horizontal and vertical propaganda refer to the ways in which propaganda is spread, on a line from the leader to the masses, or rather across groups of equals in which the leader is just another among equals. Finally, Ellul argues that even though propaganda is associated with irrationality,, more and more propaganda uses factual data in order to achieve its objectives.

Drawing on this definition, the concept of propaganda that will be used in this book is one that implies the systematic and continuous manipulation of information, through the utilization of different media available, in order to educate a certain group with the aim of creating certain beliefs and generating a specific pattern of behaviour. The concepts of horizontal and sociological propaganda, as stated above, will also be useful in the analysis of Heracles' case.

Having defined the concept of propaganda, in the context of antiquity, we are now in a position to discuss the circumstances of fifth-century Athens to explore the problems and potential for its application.

There is a problem specific to fifth-century Athens: the source of propaganda. Even if we accept the existence of propaganda in the ancient world, it is far easier to apply the model to the Athens of the tyrants or to imperial Rome, where an organized source of information and power can be easily located. The use of propaganda in democratic Athens is more challenging, not only because modern preconceptions lead us to associate propaganda with totalitarian regimes, which means that we tend to avoid applying it to a democratic one, but also because we are faced with the need to postulate that propaganda can emerge from a community as well as from a small group of people or a Cabinet.

We should return to Ellul's category of sociological propaganda as being a group expression in order to 'integrate its members' and 'spread its style of life', and recover Yates' (2019) idea, stated in the Introduction, on the necessity for propagation of shared identities within larger communities. I believe that both the concept of sociological and integration propaganda apply to democratic Athens: as we will explore later in this section, the Athenians used manipulation of information in order to promote a communal identity and to justify the power of the totality of the citizens.

At one moment or another in their lives, the vast majority of Athenian citizens would have had a public role. Agency plays a big part in Athenian democracy; the citizens are not divided between the agents and the subjects: virtually all of them at some point in their lives would be both. Therefore, ideology is not imposed on the citizens, the citizens are part of the ideology as they are part of the city and the city's institutions. I would not like to downsize the power of aristocratic individuals in the ruling of the city, nor would I say that all citizens were in fact equal. We know for certain that throughout the fifth century, major decisions were greatly influenced by particular individuals. But that does not mean that the masses were stripped of power. The masses were a big part of the city, indeed they made part of every major institution, were the blood of democracy and had the power and the opportunity to help create the ideology and image of the city.

The Athenians also had available a ready-made material for propaganda: myth. It is important to clarify the relevance of myth in fifth-century Athens.

Myth was plastic and omnipresent. It was a great source of symbolism; it helped the Athenians to shape their own vision of the world and themselves. Myth was part of everyday life. The question about Greeks and their myths is not so much if Greeks believed in them as how much of their lives was in fact shaped by myth. And myth was widely used in Athenian propaganda or: as Parker says, while some myths, even when used politically, did not innately belong to a city, as they could take place anywhere, Attic myths were 'almost all intrinsically Attic, in that the city's origins and institutions form their subject' (1987: 187). This makes Athenian myths more visibly political.

What Parker is underlining here is a clear distinction between Athenian myth and myths in other cities. The Athenians, maybe due to the lack of great Homeric heroes, created a mythology that belonged very much to themselves, most of their created myths, (like Cecrops or Erechtheus), were related to the Athenian institutions, at the same time they appropriated general Hellenic myths to talk about their realities, as is the case with Theseus. Even most of the myths that already belonged to Athens were used in the fifth century for political reasons. To give an example, I would like to explore the Athenian idea of autochthony. This was used to justify the democracy and the right of Athenians to rule their own land. Loraux, in her studies, consistently demonstrates that the Athenians did have a mythological system that underlined their autochthony, their kinship with the Ionians and, therefore, their right to the ἀρχή, or rule over the Delian League.[26] And the author also proves that their diffusion was not random or occasional, but systematic and made by all available means of communication (Loraux 2000: 34). The physical space of the Acropolis, for example, would provide a constant reminder of the mythical origins of Athens, like the dispute of Athena and Poseidon or the birth of Ericthonius:[27] myth and architecture were related on the Acropolis in order to produce a visual system that justifies Athenian autochthonic origins and therefore their right to the land. And this utilization of myths, for example, lasted long enough in time to form some of the core topics of fifth- and fourth-century Athenian oratory.[28]

And these ideas were indeed omnipresent. As Loraux describes, there was no escape from the physical space of Athens, it was marked by ideology, by representations of mythological figures fundamental to the discourse Athens had about herself (like Cecrops or Erechtheus), and also marked by the religious calendar, linking many parts of the city with particular festivities or processions:

> At every step stood heroic figures, in every corner tales of myth; in fact going for a relaxation stroll was probably not an easy thing to do, because no space is less neutral than that of the city.
>
> 2000: 35-6

It is notable that Loraux avoids the term propaganda, but if we use Ellul's categories, what we detect here is a total, lasting and organized form of education, directed to a group of people as a mass and as individuals in order to ensure the function of democracy.

As stated in the Introduction, one of the problems with the analysis of propaganda is the idea that propaganda consists of a non-desired manipulation of the masses by some elites. That propaganda deals with manipulation of information does not necessarily mean that it implies the manipulation of people. In fact, Ellul suggests that sometimes propaganda is the answer to a deep desire of the individual, a way to help him understand himself and his position in the world (1973: 138).

Propaganda is not necessarily imposed; it can spring from the necessity of the individual and the community to make sense of reality, to conform individual facts to a larger system of ideas and beliefs, to reassure a certain order.[29]

One of the best examples of this in ancient democratic Athens is the case of Harmodius and Aristogeiton. In 514, as the result of a love affair, Harmodius and Aristogeiton plotted to kill Hipparchus, the younger brother of the tyrant Hippias. As soon as they had carried out their crime they were caught and killed. Hippias kept his rule as tyrant of Athens for four years until eventually some exiled clans, with the help of Sparta, overthrew him. Harmodius and Aristogeiton became known as tyrant-slayers, received a group statue in the Agora and had established cult as heroes in the Cerameicos. Thucydides claims that the Athenians were deceived by the title 'tyrant-slayers' (Thuc. 1.20).

For Thucydides the explanation is: the Athenians thought Hipparchus was the tyrant, so they created this cult. The evidence, though, suggests that the cult was instituted not long after the deposition of Hippias.[30] It is impossible that in five years all the Athenians had forgotten what had happened. Harmodius and

Aristogeiton were dead by 508/7 when Athens was proclaimed a democracy. The other available account, which was far closer to what really happened, declared that Athens was a democracy by means of the Spartan king's help. It is not hard to understand why the Athenians chose the Harmodius and Aristogeiton version. In this episode, we clearly see the way manipulation of facts can be used, not exactly in a deceptive way, but as a conscientious attempt to reframe history, to proclaim a certain self-fashionable image of the self and to create bonds within a certain group. As Taylor points out:

> The mere fact of the existence of a hero cult of Harmodius and Aristogeiton is fascinating. For apparently the ancient institution of the hero cult was employed in this instance in fifth century Athens for political purposes in order to reinforce patriotic feelings. It is important to emphasize here that the religious observances in question were not purely proforma exercises.
>
> 1991: 8

For the Athenians, myth and history merged to create a new reality, closer to the idea they had of themselves. The deeds of the Athenians in Salamis and Marathon were as important to the Athenians as their deeds with the Heraclidae.

These deeds belonged to what Loraux calls the 'Athenian history of Athens' which of course was not the plain historical truth, but retained whatever was useful to underline and expand the idea that the Athenians had of themselves (2006: 171). In this way of creating an image of oneself, myth was highly politicized. It is important to note, though, that readings and appropriations of myth in general and specific myths in particular by any politician or policy were never final. Myths were reframed to adapt to specific occasions and ideas, but they outlasted those occasions. Calame, for example, shows in his analysis of the foundation myths of Cyrene, that the myth is reoriented in order to fit its function in a determined context. Such reframings are utterly pragmatic with a mainly functional connection to the circumstances.[31] Main political events in Athens were underlined by myth, and new myths were created or promoted to help frame events into the Athenian narrative. The ten tribes of Cleisthenes and the new Acropolis of Pericles with the catalogue of myths that presented Athens as the saviour of Greece are good examples, but not the only ones.

Wilson points out that, contrary to other Hellenic cities, namely Thebes, the institution of *khoregia* in Athens was developed in such a way that we can speak of a 'democratization' of the chorus (2000: 22–6).

We somehow believe, or would like to believe, that smart people do not follow propaganda. We are not the first ones to think like that: Herodotus and Thucydides, in the case of Peisistratus and Athena and of the Tyrannicides, both could not believe how the Athenians fell for such obvious manipulations of truth. But as we have seen the actual Athenian community could have been involved in this manipulation. As Sinos (1998) points out, the cultural, religious and political context would allow a dialogue between Peisistratus' performance and the Athenian citizens. The same happened with the Tyrannicides as the Athenians were ready see them as cult heroes and accept this official discourse about the fall of tyranny.

As Kennedy points out, even the display of the annual tribute in the theatre could have different readings by different members of the audience: 'while it could arouse a sense of pride and power in an Athenian, an ally could see their servitude, or be glad to be bound in such a powerful alliance' (2009: 3–4). Kennedy also highlights how perceptions shifted during the fifth century: 'While submission to the Persians wasn't thinkable in the 490s and 480s, submission to the Athenians came to be expected in the 430s' (p. 9).

Despite this nuanced and complex narrative, the author also defends the idea that culture draws from patriotic and political perceptions to create and reinforce a communal identity, normally created in contrast with 'other' identities that are seen as antagonistic, making culture inherently chauvinistic:

> Embedded within any work of art will be the norms and attitudes of the members of the society that produced it. When the work is promoted, performed, or disseminated among those within the community, it fosters chauvinism. When presented to outside communities it serves to spread and promote those norms as superior and desirable to others. Furthermore because both imperialism and culture are frequently attached to and promote a patriotic vision of a community, they are also about recreating that community's identity elsewhere. Tragedy, as a public art form that was closely identified with Athens specifically, and performed not only for Athenians but for allies and other foreigners, served the interests of empire by promoting a certain version of Athenian identity as Athenocentric, pan-Ionian, and pan-Hellenic.
>
> p. 10

Going back to our definition of propaganda as the systematic and continuous manipulation of information, through the utilization of the different media available, in order to educate a certain group with the aim of creating certain beliefs and generating a specific pattern of behaviour, I think we can, based on the examples above, safely say that this was in full practice in democratic Athens. Myth and history were manipulated by the polis in order to inform the citizens in such a way that they would support democracy and the role of Athens in Greece. Therefore, a systematic approach to propaganda, through the ideology that supports it and its manifestations in all media is absolutely necessary and can help establish a clearer image of the relations between politics, ideology and culture.

Athenian myth

The myth of Athens: one day, in the Athenian Acropolis, Hephaestus, filled with passion, tried to get hold of Athena. The virgin goddess was quick enough to avoid the rape but not to avoid the seed of the god to fall on her thigh. Disgusted, the goddess cleaned herself with a piece of wool, which she then threw on the ground. The earth gave birth to Erichthonius and entrusted him to Athena, who adopted the child and entrusted the children of Cecrops into his care.

What seems to be a story of lust and desire is in fact the most important myth of the Athenians. Erichthonius is the founding father of the Athenians, and being born of the earth, grants him a very special place in Athenian ideology. Plato, in fact, argues that if one were to found a city, the first thing to do is to make your citizens believe they actually came out of the very land they inhabit (*Rep.* 414 d–e). As we have seen, this myth was fundamental to Athenian ideology.

Being autochthonous means having the same rights, being equal and being lawfully bound to the land.[32] This particular idea, that underlined the fact that Attica had always been inhabited by Athenians, might have been a fifth-century creation, and it was particularly important during the second half of the century.[33]

First and foremost, Athens is the place of autochthony. The Athenians were born from the earth. They were the children in the care of Athena herself. That myth gave them at the same time the right to claim the land of Attica, being born from the earth they had naturally the legal right for that same earth. And it gave them the idea of *isonomia*, being born from the earth made all of them brothers, therefore bearing the same legal rights. Ultimately Athens is the place for democracy because of its unique tale of autochthony.[34]

Athens is also the place for justice. Kennedy argues how the goddess of the city is often associated with justice and how the city sees itself as the guardian of justice.[35] She analyses how this idea crosses a few very important myths in the Athenian ideological system, namely in the Aeschylean adaptation of the myth of Orestes and in the myth of the capture of Troy as displayed in the Agora, to give two examples. Actually, Athens prided itself on having a legal system open to any Greek who would like to have access to it, and sometimes brought back to Athens cases that were actually under an allied city jurisdiction.[36]

Boedecker has noted that there were a few myths that shaped Athenian ideology and the idea the city had of itself. One of the main topics was, of course, autochthony: the first king of Athens, Erichthonius, was born from the earth of Athens itself. Another example is the myth of Theseus protecting his friends and allies and giving the gifts of agriculture from Demeter to the entire world through Eleusis and the hero Triptolemos.[37] Athens is therefore the guardian city of equality, democracy and justice. She is proud to see herself as the ultimate place of refuge for suppliants. It is the city with a reputation for tolerance, which generated the sarcastic Spartan saying: 'In Athens anything is fine!'[38] This topic is recurrent in Athenian rhetoric.[39]

But ideology was not only circumscribed to myths and rhetoric. Myth and ideology shaped religion, architecture, pottery, even the institutions of the Athenians. The political perceptions of the Athenians were shaped by their ideology and institutions, like the tribunals, and these institutions were themselves shaped by the ideology and the perceptions of the citizens, even more so in a direct democracy where all the citizens had, at some point in their lives, a place within one of their city's institutions.[40]

For example, Loraux has demonstrated how myth and architecture on the Acropolis are closely related to produce a system that justifies the Athenians as autochthonous and how the iconography is used in the Euripidean *Ion*.[41]

We owe to Euripides the development into full tragedies of ideological examples like Ion himself, or the Heraclidae, to whom help was provided in rescuing from Thebes the corpses of their dead relatives. Also, to him do we owe an encomium of Athens (*Supplices* 428–62) maybe only comparable to the Pericles' Funeral Speech (Thuc. 2.37.1) that presents much of what shaped the Athenian imagination: a city of equality and freedom. The second half of the fifth century, mainly by the hand of Pericles sees a big development in Athenian ideology and in the use of ideology to justify the empire 'underpinning Athenian power and superiority and ensure Athens's place in history'.[42]

Athenian autochthony and democracy: The problem with aristocracy

The construction of the Athenian identity and ideology is certainly a very complex and multilayered narrative, however one of the main strains of fifth-century Athens is democracy and the tensions created by the role of aristocratic families within this new political model. In Athens the idea of democracy is closely linked with the ideas of autochthony and isonomy.

In the first place, by the beginning of the fifth century, Athens saw a series of revolutions and constitutional reforms that ultimately led to the institution of democracy. This was not a straightforward process, of course, and it took some decades to achieve the democracy we normally talk about in the fifth century. One of the main problems of this new-born democracy was how to deal with aristocracy. Aristocracy used to have a huge role in Athenian politics, and was not eliminated, on the contrary, it had to be incorporated into the need for a democratic city. One of the sources of tension in the new democratic city was the polis versus the family, the citizen versus the aristocrat. Athens had various ways to deal with that tension. There are mainly two ways of dealing with this question – on the one hand, to make sure that the aristocratic wealth and power were used for the benefit of the whole city, and on the other hand to ensure that the city had legal mechanisms to expel any aristocrats who were gaining too much power.

The first way of dealing with this question is quite visible in things like the *khoregia* or the creation of *thesauroi* (treasuries) in the Panhellenic sanctuaries.

By doing these things, private wealth was incorporated into the democratic city and could benefit not only those who were wealthy but also the majority of the population. In the first case, the money of the aristocrats was used to fund public and democratic festivals, the entertainment of the city was sponsored by the wealthy of the city. The first one made sure the wealth was the partially redistributed and created the conditions for the individual interests to benefit the whole community.[43] The second one made sure the city had a way to get rid of any individual who was a menace to the community. But these were not the only two ways, tragedy may have had a role to play, too.[44] Even in the ἀγῶνες, typically aristocratic yet too fundamental to Greek culture to be despised by democracy, Athens finds a compromise, as Osborne has noted:

> Democratic Athens (…) minimised the dangers of competitions in two ways: prizes were given to second, third and fourth place men as well as to winners; and competition was organized in more or less arbitrary groups.
> 2010: 333

This diluted the glory from the individual and the clan to the benefit of the city. In the case of the *thesauroi*, the riches that were given to the gods were no longer private but reflected the wealth of the city and the piety of their citizens. It is quite important to understand that this tension between the aristocrats and the democratic city was not resolved at any point, and aristocratic power survived and thrived through these mechanisms, yet much of this tension was used to fuel democracy.

Athens had, of course, the second and ultimate way of dealing with the aristocratic menace: the institution of ostracism. The excessive power of the individual was always considered as a threat to the community, and this danger has to be addressed in every way possible.

Recent bibliography, namely Fisher and Van Wees (2015) and Evans (2017), have suggested a move from the problematic concept of aristocracy to a more general expression like 'mass' and 'elite'. While this approach might have many benefits in order to present a more realistic social picture of the ancient world, when discussing literature and ideology, mass and elites fail to capture some of the nuances of a complex construction. When considering aristocracy, more than stating a social reality, this book aims to analyse the ways in which the epic heroes, with their values and idiosyncrasies, were integrated and discussed within an Athenian democratic context.

Haubold suggests a reconceptualization of the Homeric poems as related to their performance at the Panathenaica and how the political and religious context helps to reframe the figure of the hero and assimilates the Homeric *laos* to the attic *leos* (2000: 184–90).[45] The author suggests that the pair 'shepperd – *laos*', so relevant in Homer, loses its appeal outside of epic poetry because this structure is reinterpreted as one that can be 'solved by social change', therefore the *laoi* 'become the "founding people", a group that aetiologically predates social progress'.[46]

Despite these 'social changes', aristocracy is defined by a perpetuation of some heroic values crystalized in the way most families traced their genealogy to heroic and divine ancestors.[47] This is further complicated in Athenian democracy where, after the Cleisthenes reforms, all the ten tribes could claim descendance from the (eponymous) heroes. Robinson has argued that, rather than a creation of the elite given to the demos of Attica, democracy involved a shift in the perception of self by the demos and their relationship with the elite (2008: 107–8, see also 96). This shift was neither immediate nor complete, rather it created social tensions that played an important role throughout the whole of the fifth century.

As we have seen just above, Athenian democracy may attempt to elevate all of its citizens to an 'aristocratic standard' by claiming a collective heroic or divine ascendency, but, at the same time put in place a series of systems that are intended to control the power of the elites with their traditional aristocratic status. This tension is visible in Attic tragedy where the heroes who embody these aristocratic values are at once the centre of attention and the problematic factor within the plays. As Allan and Kelly suggest:

> A fifth-century Athenian may admire the heroes, not least for the ways in which they are unlike us (stronger, braver, more resolute, and so forth), but the plays point again and again to the negative consequences of their character and actions. There is a difference, after all, between admiring Ajax's blunt warrior ethic and actually wanting him along on an expedition. Ajax abandons his family and his men, despite their desperate pleading (*Ajax* 481–526, 587–8, 900–14), so while he may be thought great in some respects, an Athenian would surely hope that his *philoi* and *strategoi* will be more mindful of their duties and responsibilities.[48]

Different social tensions within Athenian democracy are encapsulated within this idea of an aristocracy with a heritage of heroic epic values that is, at once, fascinating and problematic. Therefore, for the purposes of this book, the term 'aristocracy' is used in a way that is conceptually different from elite as aristocracy implies an implicit or explicit superiority due to familiar ties and often to genealogical relations to mythical characters.[49] While aristocracy can be a problematic sociological label, the aim of this book is not to discuss the social implications or boundaries of Athenian elites, but the cultural construction around those elites as presented in tragedy or iconography, especially with relation to mythical characters.

To fully understand the questions with the aristocracy, it is fundamental to look into the concept of friendship. In fact, Connor (1992) has argued that friendship regulated most of the political relations in Athenian democracy, the existence of *hetaireia* were, along with family and marriage, fundamental to politics.

One important question in this matter is how much power did the mass of the citizens actually have? Its importance versus the power of certain aristocratic families in Athens has been much discussed. Ober (1996) demonstrates quite clearly that – even though the tension was always present and individuals played an important part, especially by means of public oratory in the Assembly and the courts – the power was ultimately in the hands of the masses. Much of this was connected with education. There was no special education to become a full citizen in Athens as the Athenians believed that growing up in a democracy was enough of an education. Ober notes that people were 'very suspicious of individual claims to special political knowledge or education' (ibid.: 26).

Democracy is the power of the people, and so the political formation is given to all citizens on the same level, making them equal and bringing suspicion on anyone who claims to be different or better. Even if there were very different levels of education within the city, the rhetoric of the state was that all citizens were good enough for politics and all had the same value to the city. At the same time, the myth of autochthony brought all the Athenians to same level. All Athenian citizens were without exception descendants of the first 'earth born' inhabitants of Attica, and they 'believed themselves to be a collective nobility'.

Mythology was manipulated in order to justify the equality amongst the citizens as well as their right to rule the city. All the citizens were autochthonous; all of them belonged to the city, all of them were equal. These ideas make it very difficult for anyone to claim a higher social position because of a noble birth. As discussed previously, the city used a series of mechanisms to undermine aristocracy and its attempts to seize power, namely the *leithougiai* and ostracism. However, this is also made in ideological terms by encouraging the belief that the citizens are equal and born from the earth and that all of them belong in the same way to the city. At the same time, the promotion of an education that is made through the city's democratic institutions and the notion that all the citizens have the same right to be part of the democratic city, reinforces this ideology.

This does not mean that elite individuals did not strive to seize power. Indeed, they most certainly relied on propaganda to do so. A good example of this is the case of the Alcmaeonidai in Delphi. Having been expelled from Athens by Hippias, the Alcmaeonidai offered themselves to build the new Temple of Apollo at Delphi in order to find political support for their anti-tyrant cause, namely among the Spartans. Eventually, with the support of the Spartan Kings, the tyranny was brought to an end. The temple was not only built out of piety, but its construction was also a political move made in one of the major political centres of Greece. Individual or clan appropriation of myth as a form of propaganda was present throughout the fifth century.

Athens and the Delian League: Athenian Panhellenism

The Delian League was not the first league of Hellenic cities. Just before the invasion of Xerxes, in 481, the Greeks had formed the Hellenic League. But there were many differences between the two: whereas in the Hellenic League, the leader, in this case Sparta, could have been discharged by the vote of the allied cities, in the Delian League, all cities took an oath to Athens as a leader and to the other allies. Meiggs points out that the oaths were followed by the sinking of lumps of metal in the sea, a symbol of the permanence of the oath (1972: 49). This means that, different from the occasional leadership of Sparta, the leadership of Athens was seen as stable and as belonging intrinsically to the league. One other very relevant difference is financial: the Hellenic league had its financial support from occasional tributes according to necessity, the Delian League provided regular previously stipulated tributes from all the allied cities.[50]

From the beginning, Athens was the most powerful member of the League, but the allies had equal voices at the meeting while they were held in Delos. When the tribute came to Athens, the links between the League and the Festival of Delian Apollo were replaced by an association with the Athenian Festival of the Dionysia.[51]

The essence of the Delian League is the idea that the allies must have the same friends and enemies as Athens.[52] The ideology and the politics of the League were enforced by a strong Athenian naval power. Indeed, naval and imperial power were part of the same reality as the League made the existence of a fleet possible and provided the network[53] to allow it to move freely on the Aegean and it also ensured that the power of Athens over the empire could not be easily challenged.[54] Not only that, but the warships of the allied islands of the Cyclades were no longer in action as the Athenian ones covered the Aegean. This also implied some degree of control over the trade routes to the tributes owed to Athens and the tributation of the harbors, which together with the fact that the island stopped minting as the Athenian coins took over international trade, made Athens the main beneficiary of most trading routes in the Aegean.[55] As time went by, the league was less and less about the Persian menace and more about the control of Athens over the allies.[56] This power was accompanied by a strong rhetoric that was a reminder of their power and their achievements and reinforced the military ideology: 'It was Athens that built the most powerful war machine the Greek world had seen and used it permanently and ruthlessly' (Raaflaub 1998: 18).

The second half of the fifth century sees Athens trying to defend a position as the main city of Greece. This is reflected in the use of the myth of Ion, in the exploitation of examples of Athens as rescuer of those in need, in the idea that Athens is the city of salvation. But the propaganda of Athens as the Panhellenic capital did not end here. For example, the city had a monetary system recognized almost universally which made for a huge demand for the Athenian currency not only in the allied cities, but also outside the Greek world. This not only promoted a good economic outcome for Athens, but it also helped shape the city's image as head of an empire.[57]

Ion was a fundamental hero in Athenian ideology, not because he had a very important myth or a very long tradition in Athens, but because he enabled the Athenians to use the important Greek notion of kinship in order to justify her ἀρχή over the Ionic cities.[58] Bremmer fully studied the use of this myth in Athenian propaganda in Ionia, and how the Ionians in time felt the need to dissociate themselves from the Athenian Ion.[59]

Furthermore, Low has demonstrated that the use of the Ionic alphabet instead of the Attic one in official inscriptions in the empire had the ultimate objective of underlining the Panhellenic status of Athens. It is an Athenian choice, one that makes the documents at least Ionic or, at the most, Panhellenic:

> They exemplify a move towards a style of representing an interstate relationship in which the power that is being exercised over the allies is not, straightforwardly, Athenian *kratos*, reaching out beyond the boundaries of Attica and overtaking everything in its path. What is represented is, instead, a more subtle, homogenizing approach to the construction of power, in which Athens is not so much the enforcer of an Athenian way of life as a facilitator of some wider, perhaps Panhellenic, relationship.
>
> 2005: 106–8

Therefore, we can see different approaches to the same objective: to grant the unity of the empire and to strengthen the Athenian position at its head.

One other concern of the city during the fifth century had to do with the Delian league. In the second half of the century, it is quite clear that the league turned into an ἀρχή, that is, Athens is not one among equals, but it is clearly the most important city of the league. This dominant position, however, is neither straightforward nor easily accepted by the other cities. There is therefore the need to create a rhetoric that could justify the Athenian position. We must not forget, however, that this propaganda and this ideology were supported by a strong military action, namely the importance of a strong naval force.

In conclusion, saying that polis religion embraces, contains and mediates *all* religious discourse might be an overstatement, but seeing fifth-century Athenian religion as distinct from politics is obviously an overly narrow view.

Not only is it reasonable to argue for the existence of an ideological framework where propaganda is relevant, but to look at the fifth-century through this framework can give us a new horizon of analysis of historical

Athens. An analysis of Athenian propaganda can give explanations to events otherwise hard to understand.

It is not the intention of this chapter to give a complete view of Athenian propaganda. But I think we have enough examples to establish that: (1) it is possible and appropriate to use the term 'propaganda' applied to classical Athens; (2) the principal lines of thought of this propaganda are clear enough to be able to situate particular examples within the system; and, finally, (3) locating particular situations within the larger ideological system enables us to understand them further.

This study will focus on different manifestations of Heracles in the different media of architecture, pottery, religion and literature, and will also try to understand the evolution of the perception of Heracles myth throughout the Athenian fifth century. Other than the existence of propaganda in the ancient world, it is important to understand if this concept is in any way helpful. So, after discussing the different roles of Heracles in Athens, I will focus on Euripides' text in order to determine if this kind of framework can help improve our understanding of the play.

Therefore, I would like to take the *Heracles* as a case study of the model of propaganda, as stated before as 'the systematic and continuous manipulation of information, through the utilization of the different media available, in order to educate a certain group with the aim of creating certain beliefs and generating a specific pattern of behaviour'. By ideology, I mean the system of beliefs that is the object of propaganda.

3

Transforming the Hero

Heracles and Athenian Ideology

εὐεργέτης βροτοῖσι καὶ μέγας φίλος;

(is this the benefactor and greatest friend to humankind?)

Eur., *Herc.* 1252

Heracles is not simply an Attic hero, he is much more. Heracles is a Greek hero, *the* Greek hero, with deep mythological connections all over Greece.[1] Where there is any archaeological evidence, there are traces of Heracles' cults. He is closely linked to Spartan ideology, since the kings of Sparta were believed to descend from the Heracleidai. Heracles is also closely linked to Thebes; the hero would spend part of his life there and the cult of Heracles and his family was particularly relevant in the city. Heracles is the hero of Olympia, as founder of the Olympic Games. He would come to be used by Alexander the Great to represent himself and a unified Greece.

Given the widespread presence of the hero, this chapter examines how his myth is received, in various forms, in fifth-century Athens. Looking at iconography (pottery), cult and literature, the aim of this chapter is to understand the shift in the cultural reception of the figure of Heracles and how this shift intersects with ideology and politics. I will argue that Heracles suffers a relevant transformation: the focus of his representation starts to shift from his mainly violent and potentially hubristic actions into his more civilizational characteristics as ἀλεξίκακος (destroyer of evil). At the same time, he is appropriated by and integrated into Athens.

It is critical to emphasize the difference between Panhellenic and local myth in this context. Most myths would have a central storyline recognizable in all or most cities; however, it happens quite frequently that we have evidence for certain local nuances of the big myths. Myth, of course, was not static, and local versions could assume Panhellenic status with time. As I discuss in the next chapter, this is what I believe Athenians tried to do with the figure of Theseus, whose Panhellenic myth would have been, at the beginning of the fifth century, only related to Crete and the Minotaur. But even Panhellenic figures like Heracles, would have different aspects derived from political appropriations, particular cults or other factors. This book will try to articulate more widespread versions of Heracles with the local Athenian peculiarities of the myth and explore how they evolved and were used politically.[2]

Before delving into the particularities of Heracles' myth in Athens, however, it is necessary to address a challenge to the political approach that this book takes. Loraux has argued that Heracles could not be used politically because he transcended time and space (1990a: 23). While this transcendence can hardly be up for debate, I believe that the impossibility of applying a political lens in specifical times and contexts, is not a clear consequence. On the contrary, Heracles was used time and again for political reasons and it was exactly his transcendence, his omnipresence, that gave him the ability to be used again and again, adapting to different cultural circumstances. One good example of this is his relationship with Peisistratus in sixth-century Athens. Although it is beyond the scope of this book to give a general image of Heracles, outside of attic fifth-century democracy, an overview of the use of the hero by sixth-century Athenian tyranny can help us better understand the tensions created around the hero.

On this topic, there is a strong body of work by Boardman that has been updated more recently.[3] The hero was the single most important figure in Attic pottery of the period and his presence is well attested in the iconography of the Acropolis. The reasons for his dominance in black-figure pottery (more than 50 per cent) are hard to determine, Boardman (1974: 221) suggests that it might have something to do with the connection of the hero with Athena, since Heracles is regularly shown with the goddess, and because of the importance of Athena during the rule of Peisistratos.

This connection with Athena was exploited by Peisistratos, who promoted an identification between the tyrant and the hero, particularly in their special relation with Athena.[4] After his first attempt at grabbing the power in Athens, his adversaries, Megacles and Lycurgus, expelled him from the city, only to fall out with each other not much later. At this point, Megacles offers his daughter to be married to Peisistratos, who accepts the offer and they devise a plan for his re-entrance into Athens: in a carriage escorted by a very tall woman dressed as Athena.[5]

Boardman (1975) goes as far as suggesting that by entering Athens in a carriage guided by a representation of Athena, Peisistratus was presenting himself as Heracles, imitating the iconography of the introduction of the hero to Olympus.[6] This reading has been challenged on the grounds that most vases with this representation seem to be posterior to the event and that it is difficult to articulate the logistics of the production of pottery with propaganda. Stafford supported this position,[7] echoing the arguments of Cavalier (1995). I believe a part of this discussion originated in different definitions of the term 'propaganda'. For Stafford and Cavalier, seeing propaganda in pottery would imply a direct chain of patronage from the Tyrant to the artist which, I agree, is highly improbable. However, as Boardman himself clarified in 1989, his argument for propaganda was much more all-encompassing:

> [The vases] mirrored, through their own conventions, views of myth expressed more explicitly in literature, song or narration, inspired by the needs of society, its leaders and its cults. That Greeks used their myth-history as a mirror to their life, and one which they could readily distort to suit their needs and circumstances, is a commonplace.
>
> p. 159

This argument relies not so much on an idea of propaganda that is created in a top-down fashion, but on the assumption that political appropriations of myth as propaganda were part of a larger cultural context that both allows the creation of meaning by the act of propaganda itself and reinforces it by replicating the shifts in representation and interpretation created by propaganda. What is implied is not that Peisistratus ordered one or various potters to create a certain iconography of Heracles. The iconography of Heracles in Athens allowed the Athenians, and later Herodotus, to read the entrance of the Tyrant as similar to that of Heracles, creating a cultural correspondence that is later reproduced and reinforced by vase painting because it becomes a part of the cultural surface.

Whether this interpretation is correct or not,[8] the truth remains that Heracles had a close connection to the goddess and a widespread political use during the tyranny. This connection with the Peisistratus, however, made Heracles a complex figure in political terms in democratic Athens. To give an example, Heracles is practically absent from the new Periclean Acropolis. But he is too important and too much a part of people's lives to be entirely forgotten and buried with the old regime. Heracles was to be born again and this time side by side with his Athenian 'alter ego': Theseus.

As can be concluded from this example, the figure of Heracles was explored politically, despite his widespread connections. In fact, local meanings and contexts seem to bear significant importance in the interaction between myth and politics. Both his use in Peisistratan times and his partial rejection, at least in the Acropolis, draw on local politics and contexts. Thus, the Panhellenic myth is acted upon, developing local variants with their own cultural and potential political implications.

However, during the fifth century, a significant shift occurs from depictions of his more violent labours and other adventures to the hero's apotheosis and his appearance in the company of the Olympian gods.[9] So much so that, in the fourth century, the favourite themes are the Apples of the Hesperides, a labour connected with the idea of afterlife, since the apples had the power to grant eternal life, and his initiation into the Eleusian Mysteries. The following sections will discuss the evidence for this change by examining the role of the hero on Attic pottery, cult and literature.

Heracles in Attic pottery

As we have seen above, Heracles dominates Athenian black-figure pottery. The labours, often depicting violence, were a major theme in the iconography.[10] The importance of the hero is particularly relevant when contrasted with the relatively minor appearances of Theseus, who is normally connected with the slaying of the Minotaur.

In archaic red-figure vases, even though there is a decrease in the relative number of depictions of the hero, he still retains some of his appeal. His special relationship with Athena is highlighted as they are depicted together in various contexts. The labours, that were central in black-figure vases, start to decline in relevance even if a few, like the Lion of Nemea or the Amazons, still have a considerable number of attestations. According to Boardman (1975a), this decline might be due to two important aspects, the previous relationship of Heracles with the tyrants, which might have made him less appealing, and the fact that the public taste moved on from the imagery that made up most of Heracles iconography.[11] At the same time, the iconography of Theseus starts to expand, namely in his adventures from Troizen to Athens, that become common after about 510 and are a 'deliberate imitation of Herakles' Labours' (p. 228).

The classic red-figure pottery, thus, gives us a very different picture of Heracles. The labours are less represented, with a few exceptions like the Hesperides. But even the labours represented suffer a shift from the image of the violent hero to that of a more reflexive character: 'Instead of the fight with the snake guarding the tree, or the hero supporting the world for Atlas, he sits or stands quietly observing the maidens gathering the apples for him. The apples guarantee immortality, and he is often shown already rejuvenated, in a garden Elysium' (p. 230).[12]

From propensity for the more violent labours in archaic pottery, the classical hero is mainly represented in his more transcendent efforts, particularly in the Hesperides labours. Most of his monster labours appear to suffer a loss of interest. At the same time, Heracles starts to share the stage with his friend Theseus.

There are a few specifically Athenian themes in the representation of Heracles in pottery, namely the introduction to Olympus and his portrait in Eleusis. The representation of Heracles in a chariot before the Olympic gods, connected with his introduction to Olympus, is an almost exclusively Attic theme[13] – we find representations of this scene dated as early as the 560s, seeming to antedate the Peisistratos' episode discussed above. The representations of the hero in Eleusis or with deities related to Eleusis, on the other hand, are, of course, exclusively Athenian, they were introduced as early as the 540s but this theme would be continued well into the fourth century.[14]

A point widely made is that, as far as we can understand, pottery was commissioned by individuals, making it less relevant to the study of propaganda.[15] This perspective, however, implies a separation from politics and individual taste in myth. If, on the other hand, we explore the concept of the interaction of politics with the cultural surface available, it is fairly easy to see how the political usage of Heracles could boost the individual interest in the hero's myth. Successful political propaganda (and communication) arises from the interactions with the individual's interests, references, beliefs and expectations, that is, with their cultural surface.

The general picture emerging from this brief analysis is one where Heracles goes from centre stage to a less omnipresent representation, shared especially with the local hero, Theseus, whose iconography is made to emulate that of Heracles. At the same time, we encounter a shift from more violent labours to those centred on transcendence and eternal life, namely the retrieval of the apples of the Hesperides, to which two local iconographic episodes are added: his relationship with Eleusis and his deification and consequent introduction to Olympus. These three iconographic themes are deeply related with the idea of transcendence and eternal life and his initiation in the local mysteries at Eleusis. This shift ties in with the hero's cult in Athens and his representation in monumental iconography, as shall be discussed in the next section and Chapter 4, respectively.

Heracles' cult in Athens[16]

The story of Heracles in Athens is an interesting one. His cult is not established in the Acropolis, meaning he does not belong to one of the traditional cults of the city. There are no indications of cult before the fifth century and yet Heracles is the main figure in Attic pottery of the sixth century.[17]

The hero has a very close connection with Athena prior to evidence for his relationship with Athens, as seen on numerous vases and in the sculptures of, for example, the Temple of Zeus at Olympia.[18]

Heracles is no ordinary hero. Despite all contradictions and all the different shades of his myth, he is one of the greatest Greek heroes. But different from other heroes, he belongs everywhere and nowhere in the sense that he cannot be claimed as any single city's hero. He has Panhellenic status, at least where myth is concerned, from such an early stage that the developments of his mythology cannot be traced back to its origins. Although there is only evidence for cults from the seventh/sixth century onwards, there is earlier evidence for myth suggesting a wide circulation that justifies his Panhellenic status.[19]

Heracles' cult was related to youth, strength and masculinity.[20] Women were often excluded from shrines of Heracles.[21] His shrines sometimes had a gymnasium attached and were often used as military encampments.[22] His connections with youth were seen not only through various rituals but also by the fact that in myth Heracles marries Hebe (Youth) herself. Important, too, were his labours and the idea of Heracles as a violent hero but one who fights over chaos in order to bring civilization. His cult is often linked with his mythical features, as he is often seen as ἀλεξίκακος (destroyer of evil) and σωτήρ (saviour).[23] These attributes were particularly relevant in his representation in Euripides' play, as we shall discuss in Chapter 5. His cult was very often linked with eating and drinking,[24] quite in tune with the image we have for him in comedy.[25]

Heracles is the hero who is also a god: ἥρως θεός (god-hero), as he is called by Pindar (*Nem.* iii.22). His apotheosis is well known both in myth and in art, at least from the fifth century. He is not completely alone in this category, as Asclepius or the Dioscuroi could also be described in the same way. Even so, this places him in a quite particular and uncommon situation in cult. It has been noted for a long time that Heracles' cult follows the patterns of divine cult more than those usual for heroes. Ekroth writes:

> The iconographic evidence suggests that *theoxenia* was particularly popular in specific hero cults, such as that of Herakles. (...) Herakles, for example, called both a hero and a god in the sources, could receive a combination of *thysia* and *enagizein* sacrifices in recognition of his dual character as both an immortal god and a mortal hero. In general, however, this 'mortal' aspect of Herakles seems to have been relegated to myth and in cult Herakles was usually treated as a god.
>
> 2009: 134–6

Heracles is one of the favourite Attic heroes. His cult is spread everywhere. Woodford (1966) lists more than twenty shrines of Heracles in Attica – the main ones being Cynosarges and Marathon. The most important cult of Heracles in Attica was that of Cynosarges (Paus. 1.19.3).

Here Heracles had as 'dining companions' (*parasitoi* in Greek), only νόθοι, ie, men with mixed birth and without full citizenship. Plutarch accredits this to the fact that Heracles himself was a bastard among the gods (Plut., *Vit. Them.* 1.2). Not unusually, the sanctuary had a gymnasium attached to it that was also frequented by νόθοι, who could not go to the public gymnasia of the city. This cult had one of the most venerated of the Attic Festivals for Heracles: the Diomeia. Another important spot was Marathon, where here, too, there must have been a gymnasium attached, for it seems that four-yearly games were held in honour of Heracles.[26] It was here that Athenian troops slept before the Battle of Marathon.[27] The importance of the cult in this place is underlined by the fact that the Marathonians claimed to be the first to worship Heracles as a god.[28]

Porthmos at Sounion had an old cult, presumably belonging to the native inhabitants of Sounion, which was taken by the Salaminioi who settled there.[29] There was a festival here which was celebrated in honour of Heracles, with an ox sacrificed to him. It is interesting that Heracles was to receive an ox in this sanctuary, as we have an inscription with a list of all the sacrifices given by this deme, and those given to Heracles – an ox and 70 drachmas – were by far the most expensive.[30] There were many other shrines of Heracles in Attica, such as Melite, where Heracles was worshipped as ἀλεξίκακος and where, as in many other places, he received sacrifices from young boys.

To sum up, Heracles' cult in Attica followed the main patterns of Heracles' connections with an emphasis on 'the importance of feasting, a connection with youth and athletics, and the exclusion of women'.[31] Despite this, it is relevant to highlight the number of shrines known, and the number of sacrifices offered to Heracles could surpass those given to proper gods, showing the importance of his cult. A good summary of Heracles cult in Attica is that stated by Larson:

> The popularity of Herakles' cult in Attica, in spite of the fact that none of his early myths was set there, illustrates the 'horizontal' spread of religious ideas in Greece (...). The Athenians created new myths of Herakles' reception in Athens: he was the first foreigner admitted to the Eleusinian Mysteries; Theseus aided Herakles or the children of Herakles when they were driven out by Eurystheus; the Athenians were the first to worship Herakles as a god.[32]

As we have seen, politics and religion often go hand in hand. And heroes were fundamental in this relationship. Heracles is by far one of the most famous heroes. Yet, in a way, he was different from all other heroes. He was seen as a hero and as a god. Different from other heroes, he did not in fact belong exclusively anywhere. His myth was connected with quite a few cities and his cult was spread everywhere. In Athens, there were no political initiatives to create rituals or festivals in his honour during the democracy, yet rituals and festivals were held everywhere with great enthusiasm.[33] In contrast with Theseus, whose cult is clearly politically promoted,[34] Heracles' cult seems to have spread everywhere before his political instrumentalization.

Heracles is also the helper in the war against the Persians, but he could not be represented as a helper in the war against Sparta: his strong connections with Sparta would have made this difficult. He is not amongst the eponymous heroes, he is not an Athenian, he cannot be restricted to a single tribe. Yet, he is present everywhere and clearly the Athenians were quite fond of him.

Possibly, in the run of heroes legitimating power that occurred from the seventh century onwards, he was claimed by more than one city. We know, for example, that the Spartans claimed to be descendants of the Heracleidai. We have evidence for this from at least the seventh century with Tyrtaeus.[35] Both the royal houses claimed to be descendants from the Heraclidae.[36] There were cities in Laecedemonia which claimed to have been founded by Heracles. We know that the Spartans tried to get Alcmene's bones in the fourth century, showing that their interest in Heracles went on even after the fifth century. If by these pieces of evidence, we can claim that somehow they tried to establish Heracles as their own, or at least, as a hero closely linked to Sparta, as I think we might, then the Athenians were left with a significant problem: they worshipped throughout Attica a hero who was actually their enemy's hero.

Banning the Heracles cult was impossible. Replacing him by Theseus was attempted in official iconography, yet the vases show another completely different reality.[37] Cult is far more difficult to control than iconography in temples. New festivals and cult places were created, to the goddess of the city, Athena, and to the hero of the city, Theseus, yet those of Heracles remained and as far as the evidence goes, their importance remained unaltered.

This situation was addressed through myth, which was used as the justification for the disparity between the number of Heracles shrines and those of Theseus in Athens by stating, for example, that Theseus had given his shrines as a pay up for being saved by Heracles from Hades. Myth was also used in the other direction, that is, to make Heracles Athenian. Heracles is not Athenian because he is worshipped in Attica; rather, he is Athenian because he worshipped in Attica. Actually, according to myth, Heracles was initiated into the Eleusinian Mysteries and on account of this was adopted as Athenian. The Scholia on Ar., *Plut.* 845, even states that the Lesser Mysteries were created in order that Heracles, after being adopted as an Athenian, could be initiated.[38] In this relationship between power and religion, myth and politics, the Athenians believed that their beloved hero, no matter where he was born, had once become a full Athenian citizen, and it was in Attica that he was first worshiped as a god. The same people who received a tyrant with Athena, or worshipped the tyrant slayers who had slain no tyrant, made the Dorian hero their own hero by right. But the relevance of Heracles in Eleusis has a deeper political meaning.

Heracles and Eleusis

Eleusis was a fundamental site in Attica and the mysteries had a large role in Athenian religion. Peisistratus had a relevant role in the transformation of the site due to its strategic position by the sea in direct line with Athens, and the transformation of the site into a fortified outpost of Athens is attributed to him. It was not unusual for the main city to absorb the cults of the annexed cities, but this was not entirely possible in Eleusis because the cult of the two goddesses, Demeter and Korē, was directly related to the site. Therefore, the Eleusinion in Athens was created from where the procession for the Festivals of Eleusis had its starting point.[39] However, even if the site could not be changed, the main entrance of the sanctuary, which used to be towards the sea, was moved towards Athens.[40]

Boardman has suggested that the relationship between Heracles and the mysteries was largely fomented if not started during this stage. For this author, the role of the hero was closely connected with the Athenian politics of integrating the site into Attica, and his connection with the political ideology at the time of the creation of the festival is the only explanation for the importance the hero had in its mythology: 'It presented a neat justification for the purification procedures involved in the festival and the need to provide machinery for the initiation of "foreigner" – strictly and originally, non-Eleusinians.'[41] That is to say, the initiation of Heracles provided a model for the initiation of all non-Eleusinians, which at this point still included the Athenians, the hero becomes both the archetype and the example justifying the appropriation of the sanctuary and the mysteries by the Athenians.

The hero also had an important role in the Eleusinian Games:[42] and his inclusion in the games might also have been due to the fact that his labours and heroic behaviour provided an important framework for the athletic competitions.[43]

These games and the attempt to make Eleusis a sanctuary of Panhellenic resonance are important in the politics of Athens. By the last third of the fifth century, Athens had a difficult position at the biggest sanctuaries of Greece: Delphi and Olympia. According to Thucydides, the Olympic Games of 428 were particularly anti-Athens (Thuc. 52.9–14). As Hornblower states: 'to sum up, I would describe Athens' standing at the two greatest sanctuaries in the early 420s as follows: unloved, but not actually locked out' (1992: 194).

In answer to this, Athens gives new importance to the supposedly very ancient Festival of Delos.[44] But, of course, the influence of Delos was much stronger on the islands than on the mainland. The perfect spot in Attica for a Panhellenic mainland sanctuary was, of course, Eleusis.

Since the sixth century there was an attempt to broaden the scope of this sanctuary beyond Attica. Boardman and Shapiro[45] both interpret the famous vase Reggio Calabria Museo Naz. 4001 as an attempt to add to the local mythological figures of Eleusis, like Demeter and Triptolemos, the Athenian and Panhellenic figures of Athena and Heracles. The Reggio vase is our first source for the relationship between the hero and the site. The vase shows the goddess and Triptolemos on a chariot. Behind them, Athena and Heracles face each other.[46]

One of the most important factors for the Panhellenic scope of the sanctuary is the expansion of the myth of the first fruits. In this myth, Triptolemos was taught directly by Demeter how to plant and produce cereal. The goddess then sent him throughout Greece in order to share his newly acquired skill. This reshaping of the myth, by introducing this hero in what was otherwise the story of a gift from a goddess, had obvious political implications:

[The] Athenians refashioned the tradition about the Eleusinian nobleman Triptolemus to emphasize the cultural importance of Athens and Eleusis. The myth about Demeter at Eleusis came to fill significant political functions; in the new telling, Demeter not only taught the Eleusinians her mystery rites but also Triptolemus the basics about the cultivation of grain. Triptolemus then set off from Eleusis in a winged carriage to visit all the cities of Hellas, teaching Demeter's art of cultivation as he traveled.

Evans 2010: 272

During the second half of the fifth century, this myth is given full force. There is a decree – IG I³ 78 – that states that the first fruits were to be offered to the two goddesses according to a Delphic oracle this was not only applicable to the Athenians but also to all the allies. Furthermore, all the Greeks are also called to bring the first fruits to Eleusis, according to the ancestral custom and the oracle.[47] Cavanaugh dates this decree from the 430s and states it is:

a document testifying to Athens', and Pericles', efforts to remind the Greek world that when Demeter gave Athens double gifts – the fruits of the earth and the Mysteries (...) Athens was not only reverent but also generous in sharing these gifts with the rest of the world. Such a reminder served not only to justify Athens' hegemony but also served to link her allies, and the Greek world, more closely to her.[48]

According to Xenophon, the myth of the first fruits and the initiation of Heracles in the Mysteries was used for political purposes, when the messenger of Athens reminded the Spartans of the role of Triptolemos in relation to Demeter and agriculture but also in his relation to Heracles and the Dioscuroi, fundamental in Spartan myth, using this as a prototype to establish peace (Xen., *Hell.* 6.3.6).[49]

The date of the decree makes this attempt to elevate the sanctuary to a Panhellenic status more or less contemporary to the purification of Delos and to the partial exclusion of Athens from Delphi and Olympia. I would like to argue, with Hornblower, that, seeing herself excluded from the main sanctuaries, the reaction of Athens is to create or revitalize her own sanctuaries: Delos for the islands, Eleusis in the mainland. In both myths associated with the revivals, we find a parochial hero alongside a Panhellenic one. In Delos, we find the

Athenian hero Theseus, who would have been the first to celebrate the festival upon his return from Crete, with the founding figure of all the Ionian cities: Ion. In Eleusis, we encounter Triptolemos, the local Eleusinian hero, alongside the great Peloponnesian hero, Heracles, who was himself converted to the Mysteries and adopted as Athenian. The role of Heracles is fundamental in creating a Panhellenic narrative by providing the model for the integration of all Greece into the Eleusinian Festivals in general, and especially into the new tribute of the first fruits to be paid to the city of Athens.

This attempt to elevate the sanctuary to a Panhellenic status is even more relevant if we take into account the Eleusinian Spondai (IG I³6) that states that: 'There is to be a treaty between the foreign initiates, their company and their possessions, and all the Athenians.'[50] Sakurai and Raubitschek argue that 'we would have here a mutual guarantee and protection of foreign visitors to the Eleusinian Mysteries which would cover also the Athenians residing in the cities whence visitors go to Eleusis' (1987: 264–5). This is clearly an Athenian attempt to bring the Eleusinian Festivals to a competing status with the big Panhellenic Games. Sakurai and Raubitcheck have noted that after the Persian Wars and the creation of the Delian League, the main festival of the alliance was at Delos, therefore, there was a necessity for a Panhellenic Festival that could have been held at Attica. Eleusis with its promise of life after death offered the opportunity to develop such a festival.

The role of Eleusis in Athenian politics is, therefore, very relevant. Eleusis provided a place in Attica for a festival that would not only compete with the biggest sanctuaries of Greece, but also provided something that no other could: everlasting life. In a way, Eleusis represents all that Athens stands for in its propaganda: a place open to welcome all those who want to join it and a place that could give a proper order amongst the chaos, a place where happiness and fairness reigned not only in this life, but afterwards, both by integrating foreigners with the Lesser Mysteries and by offering a hope in the afterlife to those initiated.

Heracles was the face of this propaganda. The Panhellenic hero is not only welcomed and made present all over Attica, he is also the symbol of the spirit of the integration of Athens: all are welcome in Athens, as long as they follow the Athenian rules, and the rewards for following those rules are everlasting.

Heracles and literature

The tensions and contradictions we find in myth, religion and iconography around the figure of Heracles are also felt in the literary texts. His figure is quite ambiguous in Homer, he was the theme of many lost works and the subject of one Homeric Hymn. He is the favourite hero of Pindar and has an important presence in Athenian drama. Not only are these very different representations of the hero, but some of them are also quite confounding in themselves. Nonetheless, Heracles is a very important figure in Greek literature, although his presence in Athenian literature is not important until the fifth century, contrasting with his (omni)presence in Attic pottery. Therefore, before focusing on the role of Heracles in Athenian literature, I would like to give context of how the hero was represented before the fifth century.

Heracles was known from Homer, being specially related with his labours. Yet, he is not a Homeric hero, in that he is neither a character of any of Homer's epics, nor is he from the generation of their heroes. He is a hero of the past even for Homeric characters. He is almost always represented as the warrior who transcends his limits, a representative of excess and its consequences. He is the hero who fights the gods, the evildoer:

σχέτλιος ὀβριμοεργὸς ὃς οὐκ ὄθετ' αἴσυλα ῥέζων,
ὃς τόξοισιν ἔκηδε θεοὺς οἳ Ὄλυμπον ἔχουσι.

(Cruel man, doer of evil deed, who does not care for his vile action,
who with his bow distressed the gods, those who possess Olympus.)

Il. 5. 403–4

ἀνδράσι δὲ προτέροισιν ἐριζέμεν οὐκ ἐθελήσω,
οὔθ' Ἡρακλῆι οὔτ' Εὐρύτῳ Οἰχαλιῆι,
οἵ ῥα καὶ ἀθανάτοισιν ἐρίζεσκον περὶ τόξων.

(I do not want to rival with the men of the past,
not with Heracles nor Eurytus from Oechalia,
who, in the use of the bow, rivalled even with the immortals)

Od. 8.223–5

A relevant aspect of the representation of the hero within the Homeric poems is his association with Athena. Athena herself states that she helped

Heracles in *Il.* 8, 362-9, and in the Hades, Heracles mentions he had Athena's and Hermes' help to capture Cerberus (*Od.* 11.626).

Hesiod[51] makes references to him, namely to the labours, but in Hesiod Heracles assumes a new role of civilization. Here, the son of Zeus plays the role bestowed on him by his father: the role of benefactor of the world. Even his role as saviour of Prometheus is seen in a favourable light (e.g. Hes., *Theog.* 523-31). He is also present in the *Shield* doubtfully attributed to Hesiod, which consists basically of a description of the shield of the hero in the Homeric manner.[52] The image of the hero is similar to that in Hesiod:

> Like the *Theogony*, the *Shield* conceives of Herakles as an ethical force. Although he is dressed up like a Homeric knight, he fights against no ordinary opponent, but against a personification of sacrilegious impiety and evil.
>
> Galinsky 1972: 18[53]

Heracles is one of Pindar's favourite heroes.[54] In this author, we find Heracles frequently referred to as the founder of the Olympic Games (*Ol.* i.5-7, ii.2-4, iii.11-35, vi.67-8, x.24ff; *Nem.* x.32-3, xi.27-8). His ambivalence in cult is summarized with the famous expression ἥρως θεός (*Nem.* iii.22), or hero-god, pointing out his dual nature.

The shift we find in iconography, from the violent hero to the champion of humanity is also quite evident in Pindar. He became the ethical hero, at the service of humankind, freeing the world of evil and monstrous creatures.[55] The hero is represented by his noble side and his violent harsh side is toned down (for example, in *Ol.* 10, his warlike aspects are considerably toned down). Also, in *Ol.* 9, Pindar rejects the idea that Heracles attacked the gods, instead he reinforces the role he will have on the Gigantomachy and his reward of peace and a marriage with Hebe (*Nem.* i.60-72).

Therefore, Pindar made a fundamental contribution to reshaping the figure of Heracles. We find a major shift from the Homeric archaic and violent hero, into the more civilized hero and benefactor of humanity. More than that, it has been noted that the hero has a close connection with the poet:[56]

> Like Pindar himself, Pindar's Herakles belonged to an age of transition. The poet chose as the incarnation of his ideals a hero who had held a time-honoured place in epic and mythological tradition. Into this mythical form

> Pindar breathed new life by spiritualizing and sublimating the hero. (...) His Herakles was a swan song for all that was noble and aristocratic in archaic Greece.
>
> Galinsky 1972: 37

The most relevant features of Heracles before fifth-century drama are his close connection with Athena attested from Homer and Hesiod (*Il.* 8, 362–9, 20.145–7; *Od.* 11.626; *Th.* 316–8); and the transformation he suffers from the violent excessive hero in Homer, to a more ethical and somewhat contained hero in Hesiod and mainly Pindar. Both these features and the inherited contradictions will be fundamental to his representation in Athenian drama. This change, as we have seen, was also present in other representations of the hero, like pottery. The hero changes with the passing of time, adapting to new circumstances and new outlooks in life. This multiplicity of representations, along with the multiple images present in art and religion, will certainly allow the Attic tragedy to treat his character in diverse ways.

Heracles in Athenian drama

Heracles had a very important presence in Athenian drama in all of its three forms: tragedy, comedy and satyric drama.[57]

In the surviving plays, we find him in Aristophanes' *Birds* and *Frogs*, Sophocles' *Trachiniae* and *Philoctetes* and Euripides' *Alcestis* and *Heracles*. Since both comedies came after the production of Euripides' *Heracles*, my focus will be on extant tragedy. His representation in comedy is basically one very close to the figure of Heracles in cult: the excessive hero, linked with food and drink and sex, whose appetites are never satisfied and never controllable.

In both *Alcestis* and *Philoctetes* he is the saviour, in the last one he is in fact a *deus ex machina*: he tells Philoctetes, in future tenses, what is going to happen; with his greater authority, he ratifies the prospects of cure and fame that have already been held out. That is what the prophecies of Hellenus have always been – not commands as such but statements of what is bound to happen.[58]

As Silk (1985) has noted, the presence of the hero was quite widespread. Along with the preserved plays, he appears as saviour in Aeschylus' *Prometheus Unbound*, Sophocles' *Athamas*, Euripides' *Alcestis* and *Auge* and in the

Peirithous attributed to Euripides. In Philoctetes, he appears as a *deus ex machina*, which is very unconventional for a hero, underlining his role as a god. The deified status of Heracles is also presented in *Heraclidae*, even if he is not present in the play (cf. 847–66).

In Euripides' *Auge*, Heracles' character should have been quite similar to what we find in comedy or in *Alcestis*: the drunken excessive hero (cf. fr. 272b Cropp), except in this case he is faced with the consequences of his actions and lives up to them.

The descending into Hades, with all the resonances it had in Athenian ideology and the connection with the Eleusinian Mysteries seems to have been, as it was in pottery, a favoured theme for the representation of Heracles. Other than in *Alcestis* and the importance of the theme in *Heracles*, we also find this topic in the satyr play *Eurystheus*, which was a burlesque representation of the Hades labour and *Peirithous*, and, of course, in *Frogs*.[59]

However, from what we can assume from most of the tragic fragments, the role of Heracles in tragedy is mainly one of saviour, quite close to what we find in *Alcestis* and *Philoctetes*. That gives him a special place in tragedy, a character that figures both as a saviour and as a suffering tragic hero. But this place is not unique, it is shared with at least one other hero: Theseus. Like Heracles, Theseus mostly plays the role of the saviour in Athenian tragedy, yet he is the suffering hero of at least one tragedy by Euripides: *Hippolytus*.[60] It must not be a coincidence, however, that none of the plays that present these heroes as the tragic suffering character are situated in Athens or have any relation with the city, except of course as the final destination for redemption as happens in *Heracles*.

I would like to focus briefly on what has been said about the role of Heracles in these tragedies. Both *Trachiniae* and *Heracles* are concerned with the excessive side of Heracles' passions but in a tragic way, not with the comic effect it might have had in comedy and satyric drama.

Something that we must bear in mind, is that being a hero in ancient Greece is mostly related to power: heroes were great figures believed to have done powerful (either good or bad) deeds. As Levett states:

> Cult-Heroes were often 'larger than life' figures (as clearly Heracles himself is). But in so transcending human limitations, a Greek hero was not necessarily 'better' than the rest of humanity, but simply more powerful.
>
> 2004: 63

This transcendence is what can give the hero their tragic appeal, there is something deeply human and at the same time much bigger than human reality in these figures. Heracles might be one of the best examples of this. And both plays reflect this reality by focusing, at one point or another, on the labours and their violence.

Like *Heracles*, *Trachiniae* starts with the absence of the hero. Heracles is, in both plays, the great hero whom everybody waits for but who is not really a part of the *oikos* (home). He is still the violent hero, but he is the violent hero who is forced to somehow fit into family and city life. But, in both plays he fails that integration, at least by himself. In *Trachiniae*, too, he is represented as a complex character: unpleasant on the one hand but a great hero on the other: 'His *arete* was indeed supreme: it was physical strength, endurance and courage carried to their highest conceivable point' (Winnington-Ingram 1980: 84).

Therefore, the play acknowledges a deep ambiguity: the bestiality of Heracles and his force for civilization, and that the one is not always independent of the other. As Levett notes: 'he is repeatedly referred to as "the best of men", and this clearly refers to his labours, which were believed to have cleared the world of the monsters that had previously inhabited it' (2004: 60). On top of this, the play has to deal with the mortal life of the hero and the existence of a well-known and established cult contemporary to the audience.[61]

But this journey into becoming a hero (and, later, a god) is not a straight one, in fact, it has very different shapes in both plays. In Sophocles, this transformation is mostly close to the traditional versions of myth: Heracles is somewhat incomprehensible, transcendent and his death, with all the references to Mt Oeta throughout the play, is clearly the gateway to another life. In Euripides, on the other hand, the transformation of the hero is more nuanced and complicated as the progression necessitates for Heracles to let go of his transcendence and accept his humanhood. As we will later explore in more detail, he has to accept Athens and what democracy has to offer in order to become the hero the audience knows.[62]

In order to provide adequate context, it is necessary to explore the role of Heracles in democratic Athens. We have seen the importance of Ion and Theseus in the Delian league. I believe that Heracles and Theseus played a similar role on the mainland. Heracles is a hero of the Peloponnese. By 'myth-napping' him, the Athenians make a political claim – ancient Greece is the place where having possession of a hero's bones is enough to make claims over foreign territory.[63] The Athenians make two claims about Heracles that are, I think, fundamental: his relationship with Theseus and his adoption by the city itself in the context of the Eleusinian Mysteries. Both these claims are fundamental in the Euripidean play, discussed in Chapters 5 and 6. Woodford has suggested that the hero goes through a fundamental change in the fifth century.[64] I believe this change is closely linked to a political view of the hero and would have become part of the 'cultural surface' of the original audience. The next chapter will examine how Heracles' appearance in Athenian monumental architecture plays a role in these political tensions.

4

Forsaking the Tripod

Heracles in Athenian Architecture

παίδων στερηθεὶς παῖδ᾽ ὅπως ἔχω σ᾽ ἐμόν.

(Having been deprived of my sons, I now have you as a son of mine.)

Eur., *Herc.* 1401

This chapter examines the appearance of the figure of Heracles in monumental Athenian architecture and the role played by the hero in the Athenian ideology displayed on these buildings. As discussed in the previous chapter, Heracles had a strong presence in the old Peisistratean Acropolis but was almost eliminated in Pericles' programme; yet, his presence is highly relevant both in Delphi and the Athenian Agora. Focusing on these two spaces, this chapter aims to demonstrate how Heracles was used as a Panhellenic hero to 'translate' Athenian myth (namely the figure of Theseus), that is to allow lesser known local myths to reach a broader audience, as well as to reinforce the shift, argued in the previous chapters, to a more civilizational portrayal of the hero that can be used as a model to represent the tensions of the aristocratic values within a democratic context.

Before proceeding to examine the presence of Heracles' iconography in monumental architecture, it is important to consider the relevance of public monuments and their relationship with politics. Public monuments can be significant at various levels: their iconography is normally carefully chosen in order to communicate a message; they also occupy a place within a public space, therefore creating a dialogue with that space and the people who inhabit it; and, finally, they can be sensed as a way to create what Hölscher (1998) calls an 'ideological identity'. As the author states: 'they are the concrete expression of such identity, be it a whole community or of groups of individuals within its community, and their destruction signifies the annihilation of that identity' (p. 156). Therefore, these spaces are prime spots for displaying myth and narratives that reinforce identity and political ideas.

The political and cultural relevance of both Delphi and the Athenian Agora has been fully established,[1] nevertheless it is important to highlight the relevance of those spaces to fully understand their potential for communication. At the same time, we cannot fully comprehend monumental iconography in isolation, since it is necessarily a part of a conversation with the space, constructions and iconography that are surrounding it. In the following sections, I will review the general political dynamics of each space, before discussing in detail the three relevant buildings: the Athenian treasury at Delphi, and the Hephaestion and Stoa Poikile in the Athenian Agora.

Delphi and the transformation of Heracles

Delphi was one of the most important religious centres in ancient Greece. The sanctuary with its oracle was the very core of many myths: Laius had been there enquiring about a son; Oedipus had enquired about his father; Orestes went there to seek advice on the vengeance of his father and later to purify himself and get rid of his mother's Erinyes. The examples are endless, and not just in myth: Greek history is full of stories where the oracle plays a pivotal role: wars, treaties, alliances, new colonies and the retrieval of the bones of heroes. A great deal of intercity politics and even a good part of internal politics were forged here.[2]

In a world without telecommunications, the best way to contact people and share your ideas and ideologies, the best way to be in the spotlight, is to gain access to the busy places, the big religious centres, the festivals. A large number of pilgrims would travel every year for the games and to consult the oracle. This was the place where a person could seek support for their policies, it was the place to look for the blessings of the gods, but it was also the place where the person could brag about themselves and their achievements. This was the place to display oneself to foreigners, to citizens of other cities. Year after year, century after century, new buildings, new statues, richer and richer gifts to the gods would cover the sanctuary. If there was anything like a prime time in the ancient Greek calendar, Delphi was the spot for it.[3] Given this, any narrative displayed in Delphi is highlighted and must especially be considered for its relevance. Before moving to the analysis of the Athenian treasury within this context, I will briefly discuss the presence of both Athens and Heracles in Delphi, as well as the politics behind the treasuries.

The presence of Heracles is fundamental in the sanctuary, with a special focus on the fight for the tripod with Apollo.[4] This omnipresence of the hero in the sanctuary was exploited by different cities at different moments and with different objectives. There is not one reading of the myth but many, depending on the context and the dialogues established. We will focus only on the Athenian utilization of the hero, mainly in the treasury. But the hero populated many of the structures present in the sanctuary. And successive attempts of appropriation by different cities were made. For example, when by the end of the fourth century, the Thebans built a treasury at the entrance of the sanctuary they added Heracles as a main figure in a group of statues. As Scott explains: '[he] was placed at the path's edge to ensure not only that the hero was visible to visitors from the moment they entered the sanctuary, but also that this Heracles was the first they saw' (2010: 116).

The architectural structure of the sanctuary promoted this multiplicity of readings. Around the big temples of Apollo and Athena there were dozens of temple-like structures called *thesauroi* or treasuries belonging to different cities. These buildings were like giant billboards ready to display any messages the city wanted to transmit. They were shaped like temples, but they do not house a statue of any god, only their dedicated gifts. However, they are more than merely storehouses. These buildings had a highly political function. Neer points out that they had a strong connection with the *poleis* and their politics: the construction of these structures is temporally coincidental with the development of the Greek city states, although the Panhellenic sanctuaries retained most of their importance well into the period of Roman domination. As Neer summarizes: 'treasuries are, in the most literal sense, a political phenomenon: they are quintessentially "of the polis"' (2001: 273).

These buildings are what Neer calls 'extraterritorial dedications' since they are built outside the city that pays for them, yet they retain a close link with the city. It is important to underline that this link was normally with the city as a whole and not just with a few citizens. Neer points out that the only treasuries dedicated by individuals were done so by tyrants (ibid.: 278). Therefore, most of these buildings represented the community as a whole; this, in turn, was reflected on the *agalma*, reframing them as part of the city, any gift given to the god was, within this structure, not only a gift of an individual, but also a part of the collective offerings of the city to the god. The treasuries are a way for the city to appropriate for itself the private gifts to the god. And the Athenian case was particularly important in this respect. A dedication placed in this treasury, despite any individual inscription, would have been first and foremost Athenian. As Neer points out, these treasuries were used to reframe and nationalize the gifts given by powerful and wealthy individuals, they 're-contextualized' the dedication. Of course, the individual was not taken out of the equation, but he becomes deeply associated with the polis he comes from. Not only that, but the *agalma* of the polis itself, that is the magnificent building, would outshine that of the individual gift: 'The objective of the treasury would be to reframe the elites in the context of the community, the individual in the context of the polis' (p. 284). As with the institution of the *khoregia*, this was a way to put the wealth of the elites to work for the city as a whole and a way to deprive the elites of their power unless framed within a city statement. That these buildings were perceived as such is underlined by the fact that individuals tried to escape this appropriation from the city. One such example is that of Alcmeionides' offering at the Ptoion, from which only the base of the column remains, with the inscription:

> I am a beautiful delight for Phoibos, son of Leto.
> Alkmaion's son, Alkmaionides,
> Dedicated me after the victory of his swift horses,
> Which Knopiadas the (...) drove.[5]

Alcmeionides decides to celebrate an Athenian victory at an Athenian Festival dedicated to Athena at a sanctuary dedicated to Apollo in Boeotia without any reference to Athens or Athena, even his identification is made in an 'Homeric' way: he is Alcmeionides, son of Alcmeion, he is the aristocrat who belongs to a family not, the citizen who belongs to a polis. As Neer underlines about this inscription: 'The dedication is elitist ideology in action' (2001: 283).

Another example is that of Miltiades who dedicated his helmet at Olympia (where Athens did not have any building programme), not Delphi, with the inscription, 'to Zeus from Miltiades',[6] without any reference to Athens or even to his patronymic. It is an individual dedication. As we will see, the Athenian building programme in Delphi went to great lengths in order to bring the glory of the victory to the body of the citizens, to the democratic city instead of to an elite. And Miltiades would be disregarded after the disaster of Paros and his death. This offering is the negation of all the Athenian programmes to claim a collective victory: the general, alone, thanks the god, his ancestor, for the victory in a quasi-Homeric fashion. It is possible to see here on the one hand the Athenian struggle to nationalize and curb aristocratic attempts to shine, and on the other hand the struggle of the aristocrats to retain their power and image.

To add to this struggle for power and identity, the thesaurus of the Athenians at Delphi was an opportunity to create a political statement placed next to one of the busiest roads in Greece. The images carved on this building were seen by thousands of Greeks from all the cities and islands. And the theme for these metopes involves one of Delphi's biggest heroes: Heracles with the Athenian Theseus.

Athens, too, had a long presence in Delphi. The treasury, built after Marathon, was constructed on the spot of an older building, a treasury that must have belonged to Athens since they used both the location and the materials.[7] Besides this, the Alcmaeonidai had a strong role in the reconstruction of the new Temple of Apollo.[8] It is important to note that, although the temple was built with the patronage of Athenians, it was not built by Athens, in fact the Alcmaeonidai were in exile and trying to gather support in order to overthrow the tyrants. Unfortunately, this temple was mostly destroyed by the earthquake of 373, and so identification of the themes displayed is particularly difficult. Yet, we can rely on a few sculptural elements from the pediments and on Euripides' *Ion*'s choral odes to identify some of the themes.[9] On the east side, there was a representation of an epiphany of Apollo with Leto and Artemis, probably symbolizing the arrival of the Olympian deities to the site and the overthrow of the chthonic figures that dominated this spot. On the west side, this theme was somewhat developed by the depiction of a Gigantomachy. La Coste Messelière also identified some fragments as belonging to a Heracles and Geryon episode. This episode has been identified as the first representation of Heracles' battle against the forces of the underworld,[10] thus making sense within the context of the other identified themes.

Athens responded to this display of aristocratic power by building the new treasury and by attempting to appropriate the temple itself: a new inscription[11] is added to the façade of the building and captured shields were hung on the temple's metopes.[12]

The sculptures of the treasury on the south side depicted the labours of Theseus spread across eight metopes.[13] On the east side was an Amazonomachy, probably displaying both Theseus and Heracles, on the north side the labours of Heracles occupied another eight metopes and, finally, on the west side the episode of Geryon is given six metopes. The west pediment, just as with the west pediment of the Temple of Apollo, depicted a Gigantomachy and the east pediment probably depicted the epiphany of Athena.[14] Parallel to the south of the temple, alongside the Sacred Way, was a base where ten bronze statues stood with the inscription:

ΑΘΕΝΑΙΟΙ Τ[Ο]Ι ΑΠΟΛΛΟΝ[Ι ΑΠΟ ΜΕΔ]ΟΝ ΑΚΡΟΘΙΝΙΑ ΤΕΣ ΜΑΡΑΘ[Ο]ΝΙ Μ[ΑΧΕ]Σ

(The Athenians, to Apollo from the spoils of the Persians at the Battle of Marathon)

The statues have long been accepted as those of the ten eponymous heroes.[15] Therefore, this treasury is consecrated as a gift for the victory in Marathon, an Athenian gift for their victory at Marathon. And this reframes the meaning of the iconography there presented. If the treasury reproduces the themes from the temple, those themes have been given a new importance. What in the Alcmaeonid temple was a depiction of a victory over chthonic forces and monsters is now a depiction of the Athenian victory over the Persians. By adding an inscription to the temple and displaying the shields, spoils of the Athenian victory, this new meaning is made even more visible.[16]

The location of the treasury was highly important as well, its south wall was visible from the pathway to the Temple of Apollo. The south wall faced the path to the temple, its elevated position gave it a visual advantage over the other buildings around it, at the same time the terraces and the marble roof made the building similar to the great Temple of Apollo at the top of the pathway.[17]

Therefore, this treasury is in direct dialogue with the temple. Not only does Athens try to appropriate the temple, but the city also builds a replica of it, a mini temple where any aristocratic ideas are erased, and the city is glorified. The dedication is given by the citizens with no mention of any generals, the statues are not of war heroes, but of the ten eponymous heroes and, consequently, of all the citizens.

One of the main heroes presented is Theseus, the king with democratic tendencies par excellence, the symbol of the new democracy. This building was integrated into a new building programme started by the new democracy: new buildings in the Agora and a new temple on the Acropolis were built in Athens at this time, not because the old ones needed replacement, but because the new regime had to break with the old.[18] And in this renovation, Theseus had a leading role.

Theseus is the representation of the synoecism, that is the peaceful integration of cities within Attica attributed to the hero, and his victory over the Amazons predicts the Athenian victory over the Persians. However, the iconography of Theseus was new even in Athens, let alone in the rest of the Hellenic world. Theseus is a minor hero, without major representation in the epic cycles: Athens has just adopted him as the symbol of the newly founded democracy. Therefore, depicting Theseus alone would have made the iconography of the treasury mainly imperceptible for most of the pilgrims. Thus, there was a need for Heracles, a fundamental and universally recognized hero. By being side to side, the labours of Theseus are mirrored by those of the great hero of the Greek world: Heracles Panhellenism is here to 'translate' the local myth of Theseus. Athens avoids the typical Delphic myth of the tripod, which had a very important role in the Siphnian treasury built just a few years earlier and was part of the Delphic iconography. Instead of the traditional Delphic representation, we find evidence of the Athenian hero, the one worshipped in Marathon, the one who, with Theseus, showed his support for the Athenian troops on the eve of the battle, as we shall see in the following sections on the Agora.

Neer mantains that this treasury was somehow written as if it were in two 'dialects': the Attic dialect represented by Theseus and the eponymous heroes only comprehensible to the Athenians and then the translation in *koinê*: Heracles.[19] Theseus and Heracles are represented as two sides of the same reality, the fight against chaos as a fundamental requisite for peace and civilization. By upgrading Theseus' mythology to resemble that of one of the most important Greek heroes, the Athenians give Theseus a Panhellenic status. At the same time, by representing Heracles as a civilizing hero rather than a hero who fights the gods, as had been happening in Delphi with the iconography of Heracles and Apollo for the tripod, those heroes are representing what Athens wants to represent herself for the Greek world: a force that fights chaos.

The general picture emerging from this analysis is that, as discussed in the previous chapter, the Athenian Heracles at Delphi diverged from a more traditional, more violent depiction to be presented as more pacific civilizational hero. He is not the hubristic hero who challenges Apollo, but the one who uses his strength to bring forward civilization. However, his wide recognizability allowed him to be used in another way: as a 'universal' translation of the parochial Theseus. Heracles represented a translation of the Athenian values of civilization into the main Panhellenic mythology. This translation permits the bringing of Theseus out of Athens while making Heracles more Athenian.

But the Attic 'dialect' goes further. This treasury is built of Parian marble: not only the sculpted parts, a normal choice since it was much easier to work and produced much more refined figures, but all of it. This is of course in the first place to show the wealth and power of Athens. The biggest problem with this interpretation by itself is that relations between Athens and Paros were not good. The Athenians strangely decide to commemorate the Battle of Marathon with the expensive marble of an island that was against them in that battle and where the general who was the focus of Athenian hopes proved insufficient for them: Miltiades. The treasury is a reminder of all of that. And on top of this, the fact that Athens was at war with Paros during at least part of the construction of this building meant that the practical matters would have been quite complicated. But it succeeds in giving the Athenian version of the history:

> In short, the use of Parian stone neatly disengages the victory of Marathon from the glory of Miltiades and his clan. The Athenians have a monument of beautiful white marble despite, not thanks to, their general.[20]

This treasury, therefore, means different things: for the outsider, the display of the victorious city, the saviours of Greece. Athens appropriates the labours of the greatest hero of mythology and puts him on a par with their local hero. The city of salvation, the city that saved Greece from the Medes, the city that could give the god the *agalma* taken from the Persians. That is *koine*; that is the image for the outside world. But there is a message for the Athenians, too: this is a victory of the people, a victory of the new democracy. The generals are banished, the elites are reframed within the polis, there is no place for individual names. This is a victory of all the Athenians. So much so, that, once again, trying to escape this domination of the city, Cimon, builds by the Alcmeonid Temple, the temple built by a clan, a new base with the eponymous heroes, except this time in the centre of the base are Athena, Apollo and Miltiades: the two gods of the sanctuary and the general of Athens. Miltiades is back in glory, the clan highlighted within the city; this is Cimon's answer to the attempt to forget his father and their family.[21]

There has been some debate on the significance of the meaning of this iconography relating to Athens,[22] however, Van der Hoff seems to agree with Neer that:

> To sum up, the Athenians erected a marvelous marble treasury in Apollo's sanctuary in Delphi around 500 after their fundamental political reforms and after the first success of their newly built hoplite-citizen army. They thereby expressed their growing political self-confidence by claiming visual presence in this panhellenic realm laying claim to elevated panhellenic status. As far as the treasury's architectural sculpture is concerned, this expression was staged by combining distinctively Athenian images alongside images that could be considered truly panhellenic.[23]

Naturally, many of these more Atheno-centric questions would go unnoticed by the common visitor of Delphi. Yet, all the same, they were an intrinsic part of the building and its relationship with the surrounding space. The ideology of the new Athenian democracy was stated on those Parian marble metopes, and the cultural surface allowed for those knowledgeable enough in the politics of the city to understand this 'local dialect'. And Heracles has interacted with this surface, reframed within this new context: the aristocratic hero is integrated in a whole new democratic building. It is interesting that Athens chooses to neglect the fight for the tripod, one of the main Delphic episodes of Heracles. Instead, the hero is depicted during his civilizing labours, in his fights against the chthonic and barbaric monsters. This is a new Heracles, who fights within the democratic ideal represented by Theseus by mirroring the Athenian hero.

Because either in Athenian dialect or in *koine*, what Athens offers is the redemption of the old order within their new victorious democracy.

Around the same time, however, major constructions were being made in the city itself, namely in the Agora. And Heracles had an important role to play in the iconography of this space, too, as shall be discussed in the following sections.

The Agora and Cimon's politics

In ancient Greece, the Agora was the heart of the city, the place for meeting people, for commerce, for leisure. In Athens, the Agora was all this and more. In Athens, the Agora was, par excellence, the physical space of democracy.[24]

By the end of the fifth century, we would have found buildings connected with all the three branches of power: executive, legislative and judicial. Entering the Agora from the north, we find the Stoa Basileus, where the Archon could be found carrying out his functions. A little further, on the left side, we find a large building that was used to accommodate the Athenian juries. A little further, on the right side, we find the *Bouleutheria*, both the Old (*c.* 500) and the New (*c.* 415), where the *Boule* would meet every day to create the laws. These buildings are followed by the *Tholos*, a very distinctive round building used mainly as a dining hall for the fifty *prytaneis* in service. It also housed the seventeen rotating *prytaneis* whose duties included sleeping over in the building and being alert in case of emergency. As Camp points out, 'the Tholos (...) represents the heart of the democracy'.[25]

In the central open space of the Agora were the famous statues of Harmodius and Aristogeiton, whose cult as Tyrannicides and, therefore, founders of democracy was well implanted. The statues of the Eponymous Heroes, whose base was used for posting official civic announcements, also made their way into the Agora, if this was not its original placement.[26] And yet, studies on the politics and imagery of this place have been quite sparse, maybe because the Agora is a difficult excavation site, whose construction during medieval and modern times resulted in most of the ancient structures being buried until the second half of the last century.

As can be seen from the short description of the main political buildings above, the dynamics of this space were fundamental to democracy. To this should be added the fact that it was the principal place for crowds to circulate, the place to buy and sell products, the place for discussion. In this, the Agora was quite different from the Acropolis: it was the place for daily activities, not a place for special sacred days, but the basis for day-to-day ordinary life, the place where you could see and be seen. Therefore, all of these factors contributed to making the Agora the perfect place for propaganda: the politically charged space, the crowds, the spaces for discussion and public debate. The Agora was the space of democracy and everyday life.

Nevertheless, more than general politics, the space of the Agora was the stage of relevant power claims by individuals or groups, one such example is the case of Cimon and the Philaidai, whose building programme we will discuss in the next section.

Cimon's programme

To understand the place of the Stoa Poikile and the Hephaesteon within the Agora it is importance to understand the role played by Cimon, the son on Miltiades,[27] in the reconstruction of the Agora after the Persian invasion of Athens. Cimon's programme included improvements in the Academy, three herms in honour of his victory over the Persians in Thrace, and after his victory in Skyros and the subsequent recovery of the bones of Theseus, the Theseion. His building programme was not only focused on the Agora, but he also built fortifications at the Acropolis, made the first plans for the walls linking Athens to Peiraieus[28] and was responsible for constructions in Delphi. We will, however, focus on the political readings of his programme in the Agora.

Starting with the Herms and their inscriptions, the third inscription is particularly relevant in that it clearly establishes a parallel between the deeds of the Athenians in Thrace with those of the Greeks at Troy (Plut., *Cimon* 7.3–8.1). It sets a parallel between the leadership of the Atridae and that of the Athenian generals. As we will see, these themes are brought up again in the stoa's paintings. And as Plutarch himself notes, although the name of Cimon is not stated in any of these inscriptions (that would have been considered outrageous!), there is enough subtext for most Athenians to read his presence between the lines: the glorification of Cimon and his deeds was absolutely clear. To this man the Athenians owed not only the building known as Theseion, but also the very possession of Theseus' bones, which the general brought back from Skyros in accordance with an oracular order.[29]

Unfortunately, no vestiges of the Theseion have been found yet. Actually, it was for many years confused with the Hephaeisteion due to the similarities between the iconographic programme of both buildings. We have some descriptions of it that clearly state the building's theme: the deeds of Theseus. According to Pausanias, the sanctuary was decorated with paintings: an Amazonomachy, a Centauromachy and a third one showing the recovery of King Minos' ring.[30]

In Pausanias' description, the last painting leads to an excursus on the rescue of Theseus by Hercules from the underworld. It has been argued that this might be a reference to a fourth painting.[31] Although there is no physical evidence for such a painting, it would, as Castriota (1992: 33) notes, provide a good parallel for Cimon's recovery of Theseus' bones from Skyros. Whether this picture existed or not, it is possible that something in the building triggered that excursus, making it probable that the same associations were made by the Athenians. The iconographic programme of this building, however, is quite clear: the pan-Greek mythic wars against barbarians, the Amazons and the Centaurs, are here appropriated by Athens' own hero. The battles are depicted in such a way as to underline the ethical superiority of Athens, by representing the fighting with non-humans as the centaurs and women, the images made it absolutely clear who had the moral upper hand on the conflict, it is not only about war, but also about fighting those whose *ethos* is inferior to the Greeks.[32]

Having highlighted the different dynamics of the space, we can now move on to a more in-depth analysis of two buildings in particular where the figure of Heracles had a special place: the Stoa Poikile and the Hepheisteion.

The Stoa Poikile

Even if it might have been built during his ostracism, the Stoa Poikile is normally included in Cimon's programme since it was built by Peisianax, Cimon's brother-in-law.[33] The stoa is a 12.5 by 36 metre building next to the Panathenaic Way in the Agora. It is made of limestone, sandstone and marble, in Doric style with interior Ionic columns. It was built around 475–450 BC,[34] and was first named after Peisianax but was then referred to as Poikile, or 'Painted', due to the famous pictures that were hung out on the walls.

This building was ideal for any use of political messaging due to both its location and its usage. Its location on the Panathenaic Way, at the entrance of the Agora, would make it the preferred locus for propaganda. On the other hand, the fact that the stoa had no specific purpose and was well located within the Agora, made it equally a perfect place for crowds to gather, 'a popular meeting place, and those whose trade required a large crowd or audience were to be found there on a daily basis' (Camp 2001: 68–9). Being used by all kinds of people and due to its prominent location in the Agora, this stoa was thus the perfect place to convey a message. And this was indeed what happened. On its walls hung politically significant paintings and later spoils of war like shields.[35]

Unfortunately, there is no physical evidence for these paintings. There are, however, a few descriptions of them,[36] the most detailed being that of Pausanias (Paus. 1.15.1–3). One of the biggest problems with these paintings is Pausanias' description of the first one, which he describes as a Battle at Oinoe. Most scholars see it as quite problematic to attribute an anti-Spartan painting to the original Cimonian programme due to Cimon's philo-Lacedemonian connections. Therefore, many argue that Pausanias must have somehow misread the painting. The solutions proposed vary immensely.[37] One of the solutions is that Pausanias confused the location of Oinoe.[38]

Francis and Vickers, too, maintain that Pausanias misread the location, and actually switched Argive Oinoe for the Marathonian Oinoe where the Plataians would have met the Athenian troops on the night before Marathon. Hence, the painting would have been part of the original programme and would have provided, with the last painting, a frame for the mythical accounts. If Francis and Vickers are right about the interpretation of the first painting, then Heracles would be physically represented in the last painting and implicit in the first.[39] This view is endorsed by Castriota who believes that all the paintings would have been hanging on the same wall and in direct relation to each other.

Cruciani and Fiorini (1998) have a radically different position. They argue that Pausanias' description is correct and is part of the original programme. Coming back to Athens after his ostracism, Cimon would have wanted to prove his fidelity to the city by displaying a minor conflict whose only importance relied on the anti-Spartan theme (p. 55).

Despite the ongoing debate on this subject, there is not enough information to reach a clear, definitive conclusion. This last hypothesis has the advantage of allowing a fairly straightforward reading of Pausanias as well as the integration of the painting into the original scheme.

One of the most relevant interpretations of these groups of paintings as a whole has been that of Castriota (2005). He argues that the paintings in the stoa actually depict the constant menace of the barbarian and the effeminate , in order to show the Athenians' role in defending Greece from both. He follows the interpretation of Francis and Vickers, maintaining that their interpretation on the particular painting of the Oinoe can provide the most relevant reading for the whole iconography of the building with 'the perceived role of Athens as a leader in the united Greek struggle against foreign outrage and oppression' (Castriota 1992: 79).

The Amazonomachy depicts Theseus defending the city of Athens against the Amazons. The theme of male civilization and female barbarism is quite recurrent in the treatment of this myth. The Amazons represent the ultimate female menace. And, as Pausanias states, this feminine threat learns no lessons: having been defeated by Heracles, they still insist on invading Athens. Though Heracles is not present in the painting we can assume that, given the close link his myth had with the Amazonomachy (not to say the physical representation of such labour a few metres ahead on the metopes of the Hephaisteion), it would have been natural for his deeds against these women to come to mind, as indeed was the case with Pausanias. Heracles represents the first attempt to control the Amazons, but this attempt was not enough: the final attempt belongs to the Athenians following the leadership of Theseus.

Castriota (2005) maintains that the image of these shocked women as they fight 'real men', that is, the Athenians, could have echoed the shock of the fleeing Persians on the Marathon painting. Based on pictorial representations of these scenes, he believes that the Amazons would have been represented, as shown above, as barbarians, as Persians. This relation would underline the parallels between the two: 'What Persians and Amazons, that is, Asiatics and women, really shared was uncontrollable appetite, immoderation, and insatiable desire' (p. 94).

These are exactly the opposite characteristics to those the Athenians display, as can be seen in more detail in the next painting. The *Ilioupersis* represented the Trojan women, beside the corpses of the fallen Trojan warriors, and in the centre of the scene Cassandra and Ajax, probably before the altar of Athena, as Ajax is about to be judged for his war crimes. This painting was made by Polygnotos, who painted the same theme for the Lesche of the Knidians at Delphi. In Delphi the scene is marked by violence and depicts the sack of the city, in Athens there is no violence at all, only the aftermath of the war, with three Athenian heroes: Akamas and Demophon, Theseus' sons, and Menestheus ready to judge the hybris of Ajax. O'Donnell underlines the differences between both paintings and claims that the painter had an ambivalent position in relation to the Athenians who seem to be glorified in the stoa painting while in the Lesche they are represented on the same level as all the other Greeks.[40] In fact, this painting is quite particular to the Athenian interpretation of the facts and would have made no sense elsewhere.

If the *Ilioupersis* is generally associated with hybris, excess and immoderation, its depiction in Athens is not exactly so in Athens. The Athenians had no real importance in the Homeric cycle, as there are no relevant Athenian heroes in either the *Iliad* or the *Odyssey*. However, the sons of Theseus are introduced in a very particular way: as judges. Athens is the medium of justice, and thus of civilization. As Castriota puts it: 'Aias' impiety is not denied, but it is isolated, exceptional. The kings have assembled to judge or purify Aias, thereby distancing themselves from his crime' (2005: 98).

A particularly interesting reading of this painting is that made by Kennedy (2009) who relates it with the lost *Ajax Locrus* by Sophocles. In the painting, she notes that, beside Ajax with his hand on an altar, in the position of taking an oath, we can find Acamas and Demophon, the sons of Theseus. It is 'the trial of one of the *hubristai* being conducted by the Athenians' (pp. 59-60), a representation of the Athenian justice in the heart of the Homeric world, a display of the Athenian ethos over the Greek hybris, the moral justification of the exportation of the Athenian juridical system to the Delian League.

The victories of the Persian War were, in a broad way, attributed to the moral superiority of Greeks in general and Athenians in particular. And in the Athenian minds, these were very closely related to their democratic system.[41]

If this is true, it does not exclude the barbarian/female versus Greek/male reading of Castriota. The idea that the Athenians are the leaders of Greece in this fight against the barbarians is, I think, supported by the inscriptions on the herms, referred to above, that would stand by this building. Let us not forget that both the inscriptions and the paintings on the stoa would have been part of Cimon's programme. And it is quite clear that this programme intended to present the Athenians side by side with the Homeric heroes, to underline the role of the Athenians in the Trojan War, making them stand on an at least equal footing with the Atridae, in order to establish a link with the deeds of the present.

There can, in fact, be no doubt that the Greeks saw their victory against the Persians in such terms. In book 1 (3–5), Herodotus actually cites the Trojan War as one of the sources of enmity between the Greeks and the Persians; and in his account of the preparation for the Battle of Plataia (9, 27), he portrays the Athenians reciting the Trojan War amidst a catalogue of great mythic deeds as they claim the honour of leading the left wing against the Persians.

As the Athenians of old, it is the duty of the citizens of the city to defend themselves and all of Greece against the barbarians either in Greece (Amazonomachy) or abroad (Ilioupersis). But once the barbarians are defeated, there is still a task to endure: to ensure that the hubristic menace does not afflict the Greeks themselves and thereby ensure that civilization and justice will win, and that is a task for the Athenians and only them.

These themes would all come together in the last painting, showing the Persians as the ultimate barbaric and feminine threat as well as the Athenians, with the help of the Plataians (that is, Athenian leadership of Greece), as the ultimate heroes of hellenism. The opposites are clear and correspond to the regular *topoi* present in Athenian ideology:

> On the Persian side, we have an image of hybris incarnate: overbearing, arrogant greed for power and domination, fuelled by boundless wealth and superior numbers. (…) On the Greek side, we see, in contrast, a collective image of selfless discipline dedicated to protect the Hellenistic homeland, the citizens' political freedom or autonomy, and restrained moral order handed down to them by the gods. Athena's presence in the painting, alongside the mythic heroes whom she aided, leaves no doubt as to the issue of divine support for the Greek cause.
>
> Castriota 2005: 93

Hybris and unruly violence as well as panic in the flight are made incarnate by the Persians, as it was with the Trojans, the Amazons and even Ajax and they are contrasted with the example of the Athenians, who represent self-control, selflessness and, more importantly, the concept of democratic justice that they apply not only to barbaric foreigners but also to their fellow Greeks. This new justice gives Athens her prominent role amongst the other cities. This role is quite evident in Pausanias' account of the paintings, when associated with the Battle of Marathon: the fight against the Amazons and the victory over Troy offered a panoramic view that associated the distant past with the recent history to underline the Athenian role of leadership against the 'Barbarian' dangers. It is a pictorial representation of one of the main themes in Athenian rhetoric.[42] The idea of leadership being fundamental here, the menace is a menace to Greece and Athens takes her role in order to confront it: 'this representation shows the potential of Athens to lead all of Greece on a battle against the barbarians'.[43]

The location of the painting in this stoa, in this space, is particularly relevant as Cruciani and Fiorini note that the location of these paintings just by the Altar of the Twelve Gods would have a much deeper meaning for the Athenians, who would certainly acknowledge all of these links.[44]

The previous chapters have suggested the dynamics of aristocratic values at play in the use of the figure of Heracles in Athens and how they relate to the transformation of the hero. The analysis made in the previous sections seems to reinforce this idea: Heracles' role has a special relevance as he represents Hellenism, the defence of civilization against barbarians, monsters and chaotic forces. Yet, he epitomizes an old way of fighting these threats, a way that is not totally effective, at least from the standpoint of Athenian ideology, as he represents an individual, aristocratic way of fighting, instead of underlying the power of the community. The fact that, despite Heracles' victory, the Amazons present themselves as a menace again is a good example of the way this solitary victory does not accomplish a final resolution. To understand the role of Heracles in this painting it is important to take note that the hero does not belong to Athens. Yet, only in Athens does he find his proper place. It should not be forgotten that the Marathonians claimed to be the first ones to worship him as a god. And it was in his sanctuary that the soldiers slept the night before the battle. This painting shows the new place for Heracles: side by side with

Athena, close to Theseus in one of his major Attic sanctuaries. Heracles brings upon the Athenians the task of overcoming chaos with civilization. He is by their side. To achieve a proper victory there is the need for community under the leadership of Athens. By appearing at Theseus' side, he is represented in exactly the same way as the Plataians: the example of the support that Greece as a whole should provide to Athenian leadership.

The Hephaisteion

The Hephaisteion is a temple dedicated to Hephaistos and Athena dating from the mid-fifth century (*c.* 450). It is not exactly located in the Agora, but on the Agoraios Kolonos Hill, north-west of the Agora. However, it was clearly viewed from the Agora, in fact there was never any construction between this temple and the Agora. That the sculpture decorations are located especially on the east side and north-east and south-east corners of the building (the side facing the Agora) adds to the point that this temple was in dialogue with this space. Made of white marble, it is a clear example of the Doric style.

The ten eastern metopes showed nine labours of Heracles: the Lion, Hydra, Stag, Boar, Horses, Cerberus, Amazons, Geryon and the apples of the Hesperides. On the north and south side, the first four metopes were decorated with the labours of Theseus. On the west side, the pediment and the internal ionic frieze depicted the battle between the Lapiths and the Centaurs. The decorations of the eastern pediment and the ionic frieze are more problematic: according to Thompson, the pediment would have represented Heracles' apotheosis and the frieze a Battle of Theseus against the sons of Pallas for the right to rule over Athens.[45] The choice of labours is different from that at Olympia, disregarding the Stymphalian birds and Augean stables that would not have a deep meaning for the Athenians, and the Cretan Bull that would be redundant with the insertion of Theseus' fight with the Marathonian bull. The fact that Theseus' deeds are divided into two and frame Heracles' deeds can provide a parallel for the possible structure of the stoa paintings, giving an Athenian framework (Theseus) to the more Panhellenic deeds (Hercules) as Marathon did to the mythic battles. Thompson, too, agrees that one of the main themes of this building was the role of Attic democracy (1962: 347).

It is not clear who promoted the construction of this building. It is usually associated with Pericles. However, this link with Pericles is normally also regarded as somewhat strange:

> The Hephaisteion, though dating to Periklean times, is perhaps not technically a full member of the Periklean program, in that we have no evidence for an immediate predecessor destroyed by Persians.
>
> Camp 2001: 104

Boardman also notes that the relevance of Heracles to this building is strange to the Periclean programme, and practically eliminates this from his Acropolis:

> They [Theseus and Heracles] roughly share the honours on the Hephaisteion, just as they had on the Athenian Treasury at Delphi at the beginning of the century. (...) This is another indication of the archaizing character of part of this building's decoration. It is as though the myth programme for Periclean Athens had yet to be established.
>
> 1985: 170

A different interpretation is proposed by Cruciani and Fiorini, who claim that the building could have been part of the Cimonian programme. Indeed, the dating of the building permits both interpretations. The fact that Pericles shows no interest in the Agora and concentrates on the Acropolis adds value to this argument. Furthermore, the presence of Heracles and Theseus, side by side, echoes quite strongly the paintings on the stoa and those in the Theseion, both Cimonian buildings. The fact that, unlike the Peisistratean Acropolis, Heracles is completely absent from the Periclean Acropolis makes it more probable that this building was somehow commissioned by Cimon or following Cimon's ideology.

If Cruciani and Fiorini are right, then we have here in these two buildings the essence of Cimonian propaganda. This propaganda would have been twofold, on the one hand, the exaltation of Athens as leader of Greece against the barbarian (/feminine) menace; on the other, the importance of the Philiaidai, Miltiades and Cimon in this role.

Just after the Persians Wars, Athens emerges as a fundamental city. Her role in the defence of Greece has been enormous and mostly unexpected. It is necessary to strengthen this position. One of the ways of doing so is to recall the Athenian deeds and root them in the heroic past, by boosting the importance of the Athenians in the Trojan War, for example. This does not only strengthen a mythical position, but it also creates a justification and parallel for the military campaigns in Thrace.

By depicting Heracles, the civilizing hero par excellence, always accompanied by Theseus, the primitive force of civilization is brought to its proper place: the democracy and Athens. The connections between Cimon and Theseus are multiple, including the retrieving of the bones of the hero. By depicting Heracles and Theseus in parallel, Cimon is also boosting the importance of Theseus.[46] The hero's deeds are shown on an equal footing to those of Heracles. By depicting Heracles, Cimon is ultimately adding a Panhellenic role to Theseus, the hero he uses often to establish parallels with himself, and therefore this programme underlines the Panhellenic rule for himself as well as for Athens.

In summary, if in Delphi, for a major Panhellenic audience, Heracles is used to serve as a 'translation' of Theseus, to frame the Athenian hero in a Panhellenic light, in the Agora his connection with Theseus and the Battle of Marathon helps to present the hero as part of the local narrative, and by being framed as a companion to Theseus, he represents the way the Greeks are expected to support the leadership of Athens.

5

Crossing Boundaries

What Is It to Be a Hero?

Rumour has it he's the Son of a God.
The God, Zeus, and mortal.
Half-half. Mixed bag. Troubled that one.

Helen Eastman, *Hercules*

Heracles is a liminal figure, always positioned in-between, not belonging exclusively anywhere: seen as the Dorian champion, he actually belongs to the pre-Dorian Mycenean mythology; he is the son of Zeus but also has a mortal father; he is the violent hero but also a civilizing one. Despite his original position as a hero, he sometimes receives cult as a god, and myth gives him the unique privilege of going to Olympus and marrying a goddess after death, complicating his standing as both a hero and a god.[1]

This diversity is in part due to the multiplicity of myths about the hero all over Greece.[2] Euripides' play does not present the hero's identity as something clear but explores the different types of hero whom Heracles represents and how they conflict with one another. In fact, in Euripides' play, this liminality is strongly highlighted, with a few elements added, namely the fact that Heracles appears as belonging to multiple places and none at the same time and the fact that the hero is between the living and the dead, having descended to Hades when the play begins. This chapter explores the construction of the hero in Euripides' play, with special attention to his representation as an aristocrat and the multiple ways in which this role fails him. I will argue that this tension highlights the tension between aristocracy and the democratic model discussed in Chapter 2. This conflict will ultimately end up in his madness and subsequent integration in Athens. The play mirrors the evolution we have seen the hero go through both in literature and in iconography in Chapters 3 and 4. The present chapter will analyse the different images of the hero given in the play and demonstrate how the play explores these conflicts in order to offer what can be seen as a programmatic resolution for the Athenian elite – to embrace the values of democracy and share their glory with the city.

Kallinikos

'ἄβατον δὲ χώραν καὶ θάλασσαν ἀγρίαν ἐξημερώσας' (untrodden land and the savage sea did he tame – 851–2). These are the words used by Lyssa to describe Heracles before striking him with madness. Heracles' myth is quite particular. The hero does not really belong to any heroic saga; despite his connections with the Argonauts,[3] most of his heroic legends are performed alone: the labours are the ultimate labour of the civilizing hero, yet most literary and iconographic tradition show them as performed by himself, only with the occasional help of a deity or a human like his nephew Iolaus. He is certainly not the only one battling alone, however this is a characteristic normally attributed to heroes considered to belong to the generations previous to the Homeric heroes who, even if they end up standing alone, are normally seen as part of a group. Achilles is the king of the Myrmidons, Agamemnon the chief of all Greek troops, Jason the leader of the Argonauts, even Odysseus only loses his companions almost at the end of his journey. Certainly, these are heroes of great power and might, who fight in duels rather than as part of an army, yet they all belong somewhere.

The problem with Heracles is ultimately one of belonging. Heracles does not command an army and seems to have no allies, at least in Thebes. Heracles inhabits a world of chaos populated by monstrous creatures that he fights alone. More than that Heracles is the son of a god. It is true that this is not in itself exceptional; Achilles was the son of Thetis, Sarpedon, too, was the son of Zeus, to give two examples. Yet, they are all clearly mortal, no matter how powerful and mighty, their place in the universal hierarchy is never doubted. Heracles, on the other hand, is not only the son of Zeus but also a god himself, at least in Athenian cult, as discussed before. He is half mortal, half god, half in the chaotic world of monsters, half in the civilized world of humans. He has no army to support him, only his weapons. Nevertheless, to him are attributed the biggest civilizing labours of the ancient world. As the words of Lyssa quoted at the beginning of this section show, he is the one who, alone, 'tamed land and sea'. This makes him belong to an older generation, to an older world where chaos is still being fought, this will be explored in the play to highlight his isolation and a hero quality that does not belong in the tamed and civilized world he helped to create.

This role, as stated by a goddess in the quote above, is also emphasized throughout the play in different moments and by different characters. In the prologue, Amphitryon presents him as someone who civilized the earth (v. 20). Not much later, in verses 225-6, Amphitryon laments that nobody, neither in Thebes nor in Greece, came to rescue the children of Heracles on the account of his civilizing works both on land and at sea. In verse 582, Heracles himself states that he is known as 'Heracles, avenger of evil' (ὁ καλλίνικος). Later, Theseus will recall Heracles role as humanity's champion (εὐεργέτης – benefactor) and great friend (1252). Finally, when pondering what to do with his arms that both played a civilizational role and destroyed his own sons, Heracles refers to all the great deeds he has done for Greece (1383).[4]

Heracles' role as benefactor of Greece seems, therefore, to be universally recognized. Still, even in this case, the hero is put in a liminal position: as he takes the life of his own family, his status as hero and champion is challenged and Heracles himself hesitates for a while on what is his standing. As we shall discuss later in the chapter, like Ajax, this leads him to ponder suicide. Hence, this liminality between being the ultimate benefactor to Greece and the ultimate destroyer of his family is fundamental to understanding some of the tensions in the construction of the hero in this play. The solution will come in a revision of his role that is intrinsically connected with his new placement as an aristocrat in Athens.

The Homeric hero

To cast more light on the nature of the madness and on the representation of the hero, it is possible to observe a few parallels that are established between Heracles and the Homeric heroes. Griffin says about the Homeric hero and his rage in war that, 'Hector foams at the mouth, his eyes flash, and his helmet shakes terrifyingly as he fights. The word *lussa* is often used of the raging hero, and that word is used of the madness of a mad dog.'[5]

In Homer, the hero is supposed to feel a sort of battle madness made alive by rage, the madness of Ares. And this madness is Lyssa. Even if the word is never personified in Homer, this personification clearly belongs to the realm of the Homeric world vision.

Homer's characterization of the rage of Hector in *Iliad* 15.605–12 is strikingly similar to that of verses 931–4 of the Euripidean play. Both heroes froth at the mouth and swivel their bloodshot eyes in manic rage. This is the rage of battle, one that inspires Hector to be the hero he his, and which afflicts Heracles in his thirst for revenge. But the parallel does not stop here. In fact, words cognate with *Lyssa* are repeated throughout the *Iliad*, especially related to the rage of Hector (8.299, 9.239, 9.305, 13.52, 21.542). Even though most occurrences are, from a narrative standpoint, descriptors used by the Greeks to characterize the enemy, I believe the textual echoes are strong enough to bring to mind the hero of the *Iliad*. Heracles, like Hector, is possessed by an uncontrollable rage, a madness, the madness of war; the difference is that Hector is really at war, defending his family, Heracles is at home battling his own family. The rage in itself is what is expected from an older Homeric hero, the only thing that is wrong is the way in which it shifts Heracles' perception of reality through madness.

Papadopulou, too, finds connections between the portrayal of Heracles and the Homeric heroes, arguing that 'Heracles' revenge is designed to recall the Homeric Achilles,' the intention to abuse the corpse of the enemy (*Il.* 18.334–5, 23.20–1, 182–3), the comparison with wild animals, and finally the threat of Heracles to fill the Ismenus with corpses in 568–73 clearly functions as a reminder of the episode of Achilles and the Scamander in *Iliad* 21.[6]

I suggest that the way madness strikes the hero is also profoundly Homeric. As we have seen, there is a shared causality for this madness: Lyssa is responsible for Heracles' acts and at the same time Heracles assumes full responsibility for his actions. I think that the way the hero is represented as being overpowered by a deity in this play is quite similar to the perception Agamemnon has of Ate at *Il.* 19. 85–138. Agamemnon somehow shares his responsibility with the goddess. He is responsible, he apologizes, but in fact he was not exactly in his mind. Edwards describes Ate in the Homeric poems as an urge that, while turning the hero imprudent, leads him to an unexplainable catastrophic act that is, therefore, attributed to divine agency. This divine involvement might be a penalty for some misconduct.[7]

In the same way as Agamemnon is fooled by Ate, so, too, Heracles is fooled by Lyssa. It is striking that Agamemnon gives the birth of Heracles as an example of the way Ate rules even over the gods. Heracles' life began with Ate, and it was Ate that drove him to the labours. This is the myth as stated by Homer and therefore fully familiar to the audience of the play. Heracles' life is very much controlled by forces beyond his control, forces manipulated by distant and incomprehensible deities.

Lyssa is simultaneously outer and inner, that is, she is simultaneously an internal, psychological force and an external deity bidding the work of Hera. Very much like Ate, she belongs to a world where powerful forces overcome the heroes, where gods are transcendental and hard to understand, a world where the responsibility is shared between men and these powerful yet strange forces. The parallels with Homer are striking and were, probably, quite evident to the audience. Heracles in his madness is the epitome of the Homeric hero. The hero is completely controlled by the rage of war and blinded by his thirst for vengeance. Like the Homeric heroes, he does not recognize himself after the influence of the goddess is over. He does not reject the consequences of his actions, but he cannot see himself reflected in them. Something bigger than him and apparently absurd and incomprehensible strikes him. Ultimately there is no sense in his madness, because his madness is created to reflect the chaotic world in which he lives. Heracles' behaviour belongs to an older world, a world of revenge, the world of Homeric gods, where the hero is neither fully responsible for his actions nor is he oblivious to them, where forces stronger than men influence their actions.

The mad hero

One of the biggest questions raised about this play is the question of madness.[8] What is this madness that overcomes Heracles? Who is Lyssa and what is her role? Is this madness somehow a part of the hero, an inner psychological movement, or is it completely external and completely imposed by the deities? The answers to these questions have been multiple and complex.

Wilamowitz (1889) argued that the madness was always present in Heracles, his megalomania and his violence were some sort of foretaste of the things to come. Although this opinion has been rightly disregarded, some readings of Euripides' play follow the idea that the madness is in fact internal. For example, Kamerbeek (1966) argues that the madness is indeed the reflection of a psychological burden caused by the overstrain of the labours topped with the danger his family faces. The madness is within the hero, the labours and Eurystheus have become an obsession (see pp. 13–14).

Silk, too, argues that Lyssa acts somehow as an extension of the self. To him the main problem of the play is the 'unexplained madness'. The first problem is that the madness appears disguised as justice, but there is no explanation of what this justice is for; the second is the status of Lyssa. Lyssa seems to be an 'external, independent deity' appearing on stage side by side with Iris. But Iris is a goddess in the Greek pantheon, Lyssa is not. 'She is a personification' and this personification could lead the audience to see Lyssa as 'madness *tout court*'.[9] Lyssa is simultaneously internal and external. Lyssa is responsible and Heracles is responsible. There is a shared causality in this reading. I would like to come back to this idea later.

On the other hand, Hartigan (1987) sees Lyssa as completely exterior to the hero, who is himself innocent. And for Hartigan, the representation of Lyssa in the play underlines that 'Euripides emphasizes Herakles' innocence by having even Lyssa, goddess of madness, protest against the attack Hera demands (843–63). The madness is external, it comes from without; it is a part of those circumstances over which one has no control' (p. 126) I believe, with Hartigan, that Lyssa is an external entity, but I think she underlines more than just Heracles' innocence. To understand that, I would like to turn to the description of the madness and the killing.

As is usual in Greek tragedy, the violence is not depicted on stage (the murder of Lycus in the scene before was not performed on stage either), but a messenger comes out and tells us what just happened inside. And the description is terrifying: as Heracles and his family are getting ready to perform a sacrifice in order to purify themselves and the house after the murder of Lycus, Heracles stops and breaks the ritual silence with a maniac laugh, arguing that purification makes no sense until he has killed Eurystheus (935–40).

Asking for the bow and club, he prepares himself as if to depart for Mycenae. Riding an imaginary chariot, he runs around the house, leaving the servants astonished. Thinking he is at Corinth, he has an *agon* against himself as if in the Isthmian Games, declaring himself victor over nobody. Finally thinking he has arrived at Mycenae, he prepares himself for the slaughter, and his father rushes to him as a supplicant begging him to stop, but Heracles confuses him with Eurystheus' father and dismisses him, getting his bow ready to kill those he believes are the children of Eurystheus. The children run, trying to escape and it is the turn of Megara to beg him to stop. This supplication, too, is ignored, and he starts to hunt his own child around a column until he shoots him, drenching the stone with blood. After shouting in triumph, he starts hunting the second child, who was hiding under the altar, the child, throwing himself at the father's knees in a supplicant position, cries: 'I'm yours, your child: you do not destroy the child of Eurystheus' (σός εἰμι, σὸς παῖς· οὐ τὸν Εὐρυσθέως ὀλεῖς, 989), but once more the cry is dismissed and his bones are crushed by Heracles' club as molten iron by a smith (992). At this point, Megara carries the last child and hides behind closed doors, but Heracles, believing he is tearing apart the walls of Mycenae, destroys his own palace and kills mother and child. And just when he prepares to kill his own father, a ghost of Athena appears and throws a rock at Heracles that finally stops the slaughter, leaving him unconscious.

Various things have been noted about this description, among them the evident violence in the narration with all its gory details, filled with Homeric tones.

Barlow (1998) contrasts this discourse with the description of Heracles' labours in the first stasimon that are stripped of any violence or terrifying details. She notes that in the description of the labours, 'Physical effort is deliberately not stressed and there is no horror, no pain, no moral weight, only a colourful romantic series of scenes underlined by vagueness in time and an order of events which is not significant' (p. 168). The labours of Heracles belong to myth: it is as if the chorus is not exactly describing the actions of the hero, but the frozen images of a sculpture, like the ones visible from the Athenian Agora.

Barlow counts 132 verbs in a little over 90 verses and only 33 adjectives. It is interesting to note that some of these are typical Homeric words. An example is the verb ταρβέω (v. 971 – used here to describe the terrified flight of the children), that echoes the iconic scene of the little Astyanax that is terrified and retreats into his nurse's lap as he sees his father in full armour (*Il.* 6.467–71).[10]

In both cases, a child or children flee from their armed father, except in the *Iliad* Hector quickly removes the helmet and both he and Andromache laugh at their child's reaction, in this play, however, the only laughter is that of a maniacal father hunting his children. The contrast makes the scene even more savage.

Three times, his family (first his father, then Megara and finally his child) assume the position of suppliants and beg him to stop. Even if Heracles does not recognize them as his family, their position as suppliants should have made him pause at this moment, but Heracles' violence is stronger than any moral virtue. And this connects with the second point: the way Heracles acts in his madness is not exactly out of character, he just fails to recognize his victims and his environment.

In fact, we have no reason to believe that, even without the madness, he would have behaved in any different way if he was indeed in Mycenae killing Eurystheus' family. During the whole speech, the messenger underlines that in his madness Heracles fails to know where he is and who the people are that surround him, not that his behaviour is any more violent than what would be expected from him. The threat he made to his own citizens of destroying the palace and the king and then shooting his arrows until the Ismenus and Dirce are flooded with blood, made as soon as he arrived, before any sign of madness, is a good example of this (568–73).

His insanity is only a shade removed from his normal behaviour, which is violent and often uncontrolled. Heracles' madness consists of an excessive degree of his 'normal' heroic temper, and as such it prepares us for his change from god-hero to man.

As Barlow (1993: 75–6) argues, the discourse presents a double landscape, a double level of action, the reality and the landscape inside the hero's mind. The messenger describes both quite vividly. They are parallel, and happen at the same time, except they have only one character in common: Heracles. He is the only one who is at the same time in both places, taking both actions. This double action underlines the fact that Heracles' violence is not beyond his character, just misplaced by his madness.

Silk (1985) argues that it is Heracles' unique nature as both a mortal and a god, his very existence, which threatens to create the cosmic disharmony, which Hera fears. The phrase 'pay the penalty' (842) would then refer to a punishment, not for anything which Heracles has done but for what he is. His very being challenges the existence of his family and community, first by his absence and then even worse by his presence. His heroic value and character are what ultimately kill his family; his weapons, which are the image of his heroic status, are the ones that destroy his own family. What is really problematic here is the fact that Heracles is conscious of his actions, he is just not aware of the real object of them. Somehow, he becomes a second Lycus, by attempting to kill the children of his enemy. And, being Heracles, he does not fail and in a perverse twist finishes the action that Lycus could not take.[11]

Therefore, I agree that the madness does not seem totally out of character, in fact the madness manifests itself through the hero's main characteristics. It is not the action itself that is mad, it is the double level of action, the failure to recognize what the context really is.

The Aristocrat

Heracles is also portrayed as the ultimate aristocratic hero in this play: he is the son of Zeus which not only makes him a hero but grants him a sense of glory, even if this glory and the relationship with Zeus will be questioned throughout the play. His continuous quest for glory, no matter what, that makes him leave his family at the mercy of his enemies also places him clearly within the traditional values of Greek heroes whose values Greek aristocracy claimed as descendants of those same heroes. This quest for glory is highlighted in this play with the inversion in the order of the labours relative to the killing of the children, if in the traditional myth the labours were imposed by the gods as purification for the killing, in this play the reason for the labours is left unanswered.

His role as an aristocrat in this play has been pointed out several times. For example, Gregory shows the importance of the term εὐγενία in the play. This word is, of course, fundamental to the idea and definition of aristocracy; it highlights the natural goodness and nobleness of the class. The idea that some qualities were, however, present in some men by nature and not in others, was very problematic in fifth-century Athens.[12]

Heracles is εὐγενής (well-born), this is pointed out several times by Amphitryon. This position as an aristocrat comes, obviously from being the son of an aristocrat, even Lycus, as he prepares to kill Amphitryon, recognizes his noble birth (cf. 308). Lineage is clearly fundamental in the notion of aristocracy, yet Heracles has a double parentage: human and divine. Is Heracles an aristocrat because he is the son of Amphitryon or the son of Zeus? This question is not a minor one in this play. In fact, underneath the question there is another one that helps give shape to the play: does true nobility aspire to the divine, or is it a distillation of traits characteristically human? Being a son of Zeus reinforces his position as an aristocrat but not without complicating it by overthrowing a shadow of ambiguity on his position. As we will see, the rescue of Heracles at the end of the play involves a new definition of εὐγενία, where he fully accepts his role as human (1227–8).

One of the places in the play where this question is discussed is the second stasimon with all its epinician overtones.[13] Gregory has suggested that what is in place here is a struggle between the two natures of Heracles, the divine and the human. Euripides has here reversed the usual sense of the Heracles story: instead of a man becoming a hero, he has shown us a hero becoming a man. He has accomplished this shift in meaning primarily by rearranging the mythic material to make Heracles' career culminate in disaster rather than in triumph; but he has underscored it by his treatment of the motif of Heracles' dual fatherhood. At the outset, Zeus' share in engendering Heracles is generally accepted, although occasionally questioned. By the middle of the play, Heracles seems to have confirmed his divine inheritance beyond any doubt. With his madness and the accompanying change in his fortunes, however, his mortal heritage comes to the fore and finally Heracles himself proclaims Amphitryon as his true father – not as a matter of historical fact, but as a matter of emotional choice. In fact, Euripides has done in this play what he has done elsewhere as well (in the *Alcestis*, for instance): he demonstrates that the extraordinary privileges of his mythical characters may bring them nothing but grief, but that there is in compensation a certain comfort, or that at least an abiding interest, in the circumstance of being a man.[14]

Heracles is the hero who alone fights against monsters and gods alike. The weapons of Heracles are those of the individual hero, not the hoplite.[15] In this case, it is very interesting to see the evolution of the hero during the play, at the last moment Heracles says he is to accept his fortune as one stays under an enemy's arms (ὑποστῆναι βέλος – 1350), this is a clear reference to the hoplite, as a bowman would be away from the front of the battle. As Hamilton noted, being in this position of inferiority against the enemy, 'he must be a slave (1357), whereas the bow prevented slavery (190)' (1985: 23). This reversal represents an inversion of what defined Heracles at the beginning of the play:

> The importance of friendship and cooperation, the virtues of the hoplite line, is highlighted by a further reversal: now Heracles cannot be left alone by either Theseus (1388) or his weapons (1382), whereas before, isolation was a sign of his superiority (198, 220, 852). His new yoke with Theseus (1403) will replace his old family (1375; cf. 454).
>
> Hamilton 1985: 24

At the beginning of the play, Heracles is the aristocratic hero by excellence, the hero who fights in the sacred games, not in the name of a city but in his own name, the hero whose existence is a menace to his own family and city.

In fact, Heracles' aristocratic nature is particularly problematic, because he is the champion who fails to create a reliable network for support. His individual excellence is in a way excessive in the sense that it takes him away from human contact and into a world inhabited by monsters. And this is what actually puts him at risk. Heracles saved humanity from terrible monsters, yet he cannot offer any kind of human support for his own family. He lacks the relationships, the social network that could give any benefit to his family in the tragic situation they find themselves at the beginning of the play.

Heracles' heroism is attacked by Lycus and defended by Amphitryon. When he kills Lycus and rescues his family, Heracles' heroism seems to be proved beyond any doubt, only for his madness to cast the deepest shadows over him. Again and again, the question of what it is to be a hero is raised and answered, only for the answer to be proved at least incomplete. Only at the end of the play is there offered, by Theseus, unlike all the solutions in this play, a seemingly correct answer (1322–35). Heracles is offered purification. He will still keep his glory, now in a new city and a new context. This revision is very important because it finally gives an answer that presents itself as a solution. What Theseus proposes is that the old glory of the lonely aristocrat should reflect on the city and should be filtered by the city, in exchange for the support the hero is lacking.

As indicated in Chapters 3 and 4, Heracles' mythical persona suffers a deep conversion during the fifth century in Athens.[16] He stops being the violent hero to become some sort of wise hero, the one who undergoes the mysteries, the one who takes the apples of the Hesperides, the one who goes to Hades and back. I believe that this is utilized to reframe the potential danger of aristocracy within the democratic city.

Whenever an aristocrat tries to shine above his city, the whole city is at risk. We have seen in Chapter 2 how this was a constant source of tension for democratic Athens. Heracles is the epitome of this, by being the solitary hero, the lonely champion, he puts his family at risk and ends up destroying it. The solution that Theseus offers is the solution offered by Athens to their aristocrats: integration into the city at the expense of sharing the individual glory with the community.

Friends will be friends

Friendship is one of the main themes of this play. Silk states that, after surpassing unsurmountable turmoil, the play comes to 'rest with a long articulation of the theme of friendship', the author follows by affirming that the play provides no explanation for this emphasis on the theme of friendship.[17] I would like to argue otherwise. In fact, the theme of friendship, contrary to the question of madness, is introduced in the prologue of the play and is core to the development of the plot. In the first part of the play, the lack of powerful friends poses a real threat to the family of Heracles. In the last part, it is true friendship that finally offers the much needed redemption. Many lines of text revolve around the idea of friendship and what its true meaning and value are: good friends, bad friends, powerful friends, useless friends, all are discussed in this play.[18] This section will argue that the representation of friendship in this play (as it is the case with other Greek tragedies) is closely linked with the notion of political ties and the politics of Athens.

It is useful at this stage to consider how the theme of friendship is developed in this play in order to understand its construction. At 53–9, Amphitryon gives us a definition of friendship as he knows it at the moment: there are two kinds of friends, the false and powerful and the true friends though powerless.

The necessity for true and powerful friends is obvious from the situation, yet we will not find any of those until the end of the play. This first reference to friendship makes a very important distinction and introduces a relevant axiom between power and friendship that will only be solved in the end by Theseus: the powerful but false friends disappear in times of trouble while the true friends who stay under all circumstances are normally powerless. This last case is clearly the case of the chorus: they are good friends, but they are old and absolutely powerless to defend the family of Heracles. Therefore, the Megara's conclusion at verses 84–5 is quite logical: there is no salvation from friends. The theme is expanded in verses 227–35, where the helplessness of Amphitryon's friends in general and the chorus in particular is underlined. The theme is closely related to that of salvation. In fact, the lack of friends means the lack of salvation. And this lack of friendship is expanded from those in the city to the whole of Greece. After all, Heracles' labours benefited the whole of Greece and one ought to expect some friendship in return, but clearly that is not the case. Greece has failed Heracles.

And if the friendship of those present in the drama is useless, so is the friendship of those far away. The friendship of a host is short (303–5). That is, seeking refuge somewhere else is not going to solve the problem. And the problem has the ultimate expansion in 339: Zeus is less of a friend than he seems. As Megara highlights, the lack of friendship means the lack of hope (551). When even Zeus is absent to save this family, it seems all hope has vanished. It is at that moment that Heracles comes back, when all hope has vanished, Heracles impersonates hope in a hopeless situation: he is as good at saving you as Zeus himself (520–2). A new friend has come, the ultimate friend, the father, son and husband of those in distress. After a summary of the problem of friendship, Heracles resumes his action to save his family. But, of course, this salvation is short-lived, and by divine intervention, Heracles turns out to be the worst possible enemy of his family.

Having killed his own family, Heracles is in more need of friends than ever before. However, he is back to square one: Amphitryon and the chorus are powerless, the gods are absent at best, opposed at worst. There seems to be no friendship or salvation for the hero. And then comes the ultimate of friends: Theseus. At this point it must be noted that the audience would not be expecting this appearance: there are no clues for the importance of Theseus in the prologue of the play, and the fact that the order of the myth is rearranged (making the labours prior to the killing of the children), would have left the audience without a safe timeline for the action. Therefore, they would probably have rejoiced with the return of Heracles, only to have their hopes crushed with the characters and finally to see the hero of the city come to the rescue.

Theseus is presented by Heracles as a friend and someone on an equal footing: συγγενὴς (ally, 1153–4). However, Theseus is not exactly a friend, or at least not just a friend, nor does his help come simply from his aristocratic position: when he introduces himself, he says he has come as συμμάχος (1165). I believe this is more than simple semantics: it has been noted that, on stage, Theseus is more than himself, he is Athens. Theseus comes to finish the work started by Athena when she stopped Heracles before he would commit the ultimate crime. Theseus gives a new definition of friendship that is, in fact, a definition of συμμαχία (1220 ff.): in this new relationship, friends support each other and are not afraid of the old *alastor* from the past.

In this new relationship, the world is dominated by binding rules between human beings and cities instead of aristocratic familial values and ties, this new relationship is defined by the image of the yoke (1403), however it is not a symmetrical yoke. In fact, one of the parts is ill-fated, given the idea that the other part is in fact doing most of the effort in pulling the other half forward: this is the kind of man one ought to have as a friend, or the kind of city you ought to have as an ally, one might think. Theseus is in effect the only answer to the problems enunciated in the first half of the play. He is the true friend who is also powerful, the friend to a man in trouble. The relationship between Heracles and Theseus is ultimately a political and military one: they are allies (συμμάχοι). And it is the fact that Theseus is an ally that ultimately solves the problem stated at the beginning of the play: Theseus is simultaneously a true friend and powerful.

Therefore, verse 1225 is, I think, ultimately a political statement. What Theseus is defending is the way he, king of Athens, and therefore his city, act towards their allies. This context allows for a different approach to the way this theme develops in the play: as an illustration on how all friendships are ultimately useless unless you have powerful allies. And that would have been quite a strong message to the delegates of all the Athenian allies attending the performance of this play in the theatre.

The last lines of Heracles are the summary of the whole play and all the reflections of friendship: whoever wants to acquire wealth or fortune rather than good friends is a fool (1425–6). Nevertheless, as we will discuss further down in this chapter, this salvation is not for everybody.

Heracles and *Ajax*: Is there any hope?

Having discussed the various representations of Heracles in this play, the comparison with another hero might bring some further light to this question. There are strong similarities between this play and Sophocles' *Ajax*. Both plays share an important theme: the aristocratic hero of old who does not fit into the new world and is struck by a divinely inflicted madness.[19] There are, however, two main differences between these two plays: hope and friendship, and they are developed in close connection with each other.

One of the main questions relevant to Euripides' play is whether or when to abandon hope. Megara constantly questions the place for hope, to which Amphitryon answers that he does cherish hope, the brave man always keeps his hope (91, 105–6). In 144, Lycus echoes Megara's question: what hope do they have? In 295–7, Megara exposes this hope as nonsense since no man ever came from Hades. However, Megara is not presented as a cynic. She, too, used to have hopes (460–1), she just abandoned them too early and finally convinces Amphitryon to abandon his (505–6). Yet, the answer given by Heracles' apparition and later by Heracles' choice to live settle this dispute in the sense that a hero does hope, and there is hope for him, however, in this play, this hope is only made possible in the context of integration into the ideal city, that is Athens as represented by Theseus. In *Ajax*, on the other hand, hope is always seen as a negative: Ajax rejects hope (477–8) and the chorus can only hope for their death in what is clearly stated as a bad hope (1381).

The main difference between Heracles and Ajax and the choice to accept and reject hope is friendship. Heracles can count on Theseus. Ajax, like

Amphitryon, only counts on the chorus that is powerless to save him,[20] therefore no salvation comes to either of them.

Both plays in a sense display the problems of Homeric ethics within the contemporary world of the democratic polis. However, in one case, there is no hope or friendship powerful enough to guide the hero to this new reality. Ajax is and always will be a Homeric hero of old. As is Amphitryon and the chorus of Thebans. Papadopoulou (2005) has demonstrated that the question of heroism is indeed central to the play, Euripides chooses to create a hero who is not perfect nor weighted down by hybris, making his disaster seemingly unrelated to his conduct, what the tragedy is constructed around is the nature of Heracles' heroism, and how heroes can become a part of civilization (p. 56).

To conclude: the dramatization of madness in the play effectively problematizes the place that Heracles, the famous performer of heroic deeds, may have in human society. It is relevant to note that Euripides reverses the sequence from labours as a consequence of the madness, whereas in versions of the story which give the 'madness–labours' sequence the labours are one step before deification, in Euripides there is no such thing, and the dramatist presents the gradual humanization of Heracles.[21]

It is true that Sophocles' Ajax is in no way the Homeric Ajax. But it is also true that there are differences between the Homeric and the classical world, especially if we talk about the Athenian classical world, where notions of aristocracy and individualism could be considered a threat to democracy. Since the implementation of democracy in Athens, the existence of an aristocracy was very problematic. What is the role of the full proper aristocracy within the democratic city? The city had a series of ways to deal with this problem, namely the institution of *khoregia* or, taken to an extreme, the ostracism. The role of the aristocrat in the city is quite often questioned in Attic tragedy. And I believe that the solution that is offered in the plays is quite often the one that was offered in real life, that is, for an aristocrat to be integrated into the city, he has to share his glory with all the people of his city.

In the second half of the play, we have the corpse of Ajax, his concubine crying, his brother mourning, and we have the enemies of Ajax: Odysseus, Menelaus and Agamemnon. There is something extraordinary happening to the body of the hero: his son kneels besides him (*Ajax*, 1171–9). There is no custom whatsoever of being a suppliant next to a corpse. There is, however, the custom of being a suppliant next to a hero's grave. Ajax's body is already sacred.[22] And for the first time, and only after his death, does Ajax contribute to the wellbeing of his family. It is important to remember that in Salamis the cult of the hero was directly connected with the sanctuary of his son. What we have here is the symbol, the prototype of that cult.

Somehow, Ajax is already the Athenian hero, and that marks a change in what was otherwise a hero with almost no regards for his family. This is, I think, the way of integrating the aristocratic hero into the democratic polis. From the moment he is a cult hero, his glory does not belong soley to himself any more, but is reflected on his city and those who respect him. Somehow, in the second half of the play, Ajax is already in Athens, he is already the hero in the grave all the Athenians in the audience knew. The hero is dead. But that death means his redemption and the glory of Athens.

The answer given in *Ajax*, I think, is therefore quite similar to that of *Heracles*. There is one way of being integrated into the new democratic polis: Heracles does that with the help of Theseus by going alive into the city and sharing his glory with the citizens, and Ajax does that by dying and becoming the cult hero widely known to Athenians.

So, what is it to be a hero? As we have seen, many possibilities are exploited: the lone champion, the aristocrat, the Homeric hero, only to be proven wrong time after time. Only Theseus gives an answer powerful enough to save the hero in this new age: and the answer is Athens, the answer is to give the crown of glory to the city and belong to a community instead of following individual glory.

As we have seen in Chapter 4, this is not the first utilization of the myth of Heracles in order to offer an epitome of aristocratic behaviour: he was used in the same way, also there with the help of Theseus, in the Athenian treasury at Delphi. Heracles is the epitome of the hero of old who is strong enough to be transformed. His madness is in a sense necessary to bring him into the new paradigm, to activate a transformation that enables him to leave his world of monsters behind and enter the civilization he is in part responsible for. He is, in this play, and contrary to Ajax who could never fit in, a model of integration of aristocratic values and behaviours within a democratic city.

6

Into Athens

Old Gods and New Gods

All Gods fear their sons. Kronos, Father Time, knew
Knew his son Zeus would overthrow him. Zeus took his father's watch
And stopped it. Now all Zeus fears is his own time coming.

Helen Eastman, Hercules

As discussed in Chapter 4, Delphi was one of the main centres of Panhellenic religion. The myth of Heracles had deep roots in the sanctuary – after all, Heracles is the hero who fights Apollo. And it is in Delphi that Heracles, after murdering his children, is usually given the labours in order to be purified. Euripides has, however, changed the myth, and totally ignores the role of both Delphi and Apollo in Heracles' story. The importance of the sanctuary in the purification of the hero is completely relegated in favour of a purification in Athens. The relationship with the gods in this play and the notion of justice are quite complex and, I believe, have often been misunderstood. For example, Foley points out that in this play justice does not come from gods or humans: his retaliation on those who threaten his family is met with an incomprehensible violence underlining a 'hostile divine and human reality in which he is trapped' (1985: 158).

Heracles is indeed 'trapped' in a hostile environment that is beyond his control, he is trapped in his own pollution, an inherited pollution that ultimately derives from the anger of Hera at is existence. But the play offers a solution for the problem. To understand that solution it is fundamental to understand the problem, namely the role of the gods in this play and the notion of justice represented.

It is very relevant to note that Delphi used to play a fundamental role in the Heracles myth. It was there that the hero, after killing his children, was purified and received the task of the labours as a punishment for his crime (cf. Apollod., *Bibl.* 2.4.48–9). By inverting the myth, Euripides is denying any importance to the sanctuary. As Said notes, this is the same treatment the myth of Orestes receives in Euripides' play of the same name.[1]

This is different from what we find, for example, in the *Oresteia*, where, despite the fact that the final solution can only be found in Athens, the sanctuary of Apollo still plays a major role; in both *Heracles* and *Orestes* the sanctuary completely disappears. This seems to be in tune with the progressive control of Delphi by Sparta and the loss of importance of the Athenians there.[2] As has been stated in Chapter 3, this shift in power at Delphi might have been the justification for Athens' attempt to promote the festival at Eleusis to a Panhellenic status.[3]

Gods

The representation of the gods is a structural if quite problematic element in this play.[4] The analysis of the gods' interventions, or lack thereof, and their relationship with the hero is fundamental to understanding the play. I will argue that, being associated with different ideas of justice, the gods in the play are represented through a prism of the city they are mostly connected with, at least from the majority audience's point of view.

The very first problem is where is Zeus? Is Zeus at all reliable to save his family? Then, of course, the role of Hera in Heracles' madness is not a clear one. What are the reasons for Hera's attack? What is the purpose of her attack and how does that relate to the hero? Is it a plain vengeful act or is Heracles somehow deserving of such punishment by the gods?

Past studies have yielded some important insights into these questions, however the answer seems to be elusive. So much so, that Griffiths suggested that Euripides may be providing a deliberately paradoxical situation:

> Gods in tragedy are capricious and easily provoked to violence as when Aphrodite attacks Hippolytus because he has not worshipped her, but Iris' explanation frames the debate in legalistic terms (…). The idea of paying a penalty or receiving justice has been seen earlier in the play, when the Chorus had spoken of Lycus receiving justice for his actions (765). there is

however a key difference: Lycus receives justice for 'the things he has done', but Heracles' crime is not stated.

2006: 89

The family of Heracles gathers around the altar of Zeus during the first third of the play. And time and again they beg for protection as suppliants. Yet Zeus is totally and completely absent during the whole play.[5] How is it possible that Zeus neglects in this way his own son and his family? Before trying to answer this question, I would like to refer to a relevant passage in *Iliad*, where Patroclus is about to kill Sarpedon (*Il.* 16. 431–61). Zeus pities his son and wants to save him, but Hera makes the point that if he is indeed to intervene and save his son, chaos would strike within the war. It is very interesting that Hera plays the role she does in this passage. She is somehow a guardian of order and makes sure the divine order is not disturbed by Zeus' favouritism. She wants to ensure that the line between the divine and the human is not crossed. That is exactly the role she takes on in this play: she assures the lines are not crossed; her role is to make sure justice is carried out:

Ιρ. ὡς ἂν πορεύσας δι' Ἀχερούσιον πόρον
τὸν καλλίπαιδα στέφανον αὐθέντηι φόνωι
γνῶι μὲν τὸν Ἥρας οἷός ἐστ' αὐτῶι χόλος,
μάθηι δὲ τὸν ἐμόν· ἢ θεοὶ μὲν οὐδαμοῦ,
τὰ θνητὰ δ' ἔσται μεγάλα, μὴ δόντος δίκην.
(...)
μὴ σὺ νουθέτει τά θ' Ἥρας κἀμὰ μηχανήματα.
Λυ. ἐς τὸ λῶιον ἐμβιβάζω σ' ἴχνος ἀντὶ τοῦ κακοῦ.
Ιρ. οὐχὶ σωφρονεῖν γ' ἔπεμψε δεῦρό σ' ἡ Διὸς δάμαρ

(838–42, 855–7)

Iris so that when he makes the crown of the beautiful children cross Acheron with murderous slaughter, he might know the reality of Hera's anger towards himself
and might learn my own. As the gods amount to nothing
and the humans are immense, if justice is not done
(...) Don't you give advice on mine and Hera's plans.

Lyssa I want to lead your footsteps towards good and away from evil.

Iris It was not in order to be self-controlled that the wife of Zeus sent you here.

I have argued before that the madness that strikes Heracles is used to underline his connection with the Homeric heroes. In the same manner, I think that Zeus seams to reflect the Homeric episode of Sarpedon referred to above: from a human standpoint he remains mainly absent and incomprehensible. Different from the *Iliad*, however, this tragedy does not offer a glimpse of whatever moral struggle Zeus might be suffering during the action.

But not all gods are distant or malevolent. Completely different from the role of Zeus and Hera is the role of Athena. If we assume that indeed Heracles' madness had something to do with divine justice, Athena cannot intervene against the will of Hera. Her intervention at the last minute, as she stops Heracles in time to prevent him from doing the most hideous of the crimes, killing his own father (1001–8), seems to indicate that Hera's justice is fulfilled by the killing of the children and Megara.

As considered on Chapter 2, Athena has long since been associated with Heracles. She appears as his helper both inside and outside Athens, namely in the Temple of Zeus at Olympia. So, her role here makes perfect sense. However, it has been noted that this role is not only related to an ancestral connection between the hero and the goddess, but also between the goddess and her city.

It is appropriate that Athena should put a halt to the carnage, for she is often represented in art (in four of the metopes of the Temple of Zeus at Olympia, for example, and in a large number of vases) as Heracles' guardian deity. Her intervention here, however, has additional connotations. The messenger describes her as decked out in full battle regalia, equipped with helmet and spear – an image that would presumably conjure up for Euripides' audience the great bronze statue of Athena above them on the Acropolis, standing guard over the city of Athens. Athena's intervention prefigures the role the city of Athens will perform for Heracles at the end of the play.[6]

Griffiths, too, underlines this role of the goddess and her connection with Theseus and Athena, despite the relationships that bond Zeus with Heracles as his father and Athena as his agent, Athena and Heracles together, the author suggests that the role of the goddess in this play is directly related to the audience and establishes a connection with Theseus who is to arrive soon after Athena's intervention.[7] She is much more than the helper of Heracles: this goddess is not just any version of the goddess, she is described as Athena Promachos, the goddess of the city, representing Athens.

This reading helps to create a contrast between this close protective goddess and the distant incomprehensible Zeus and Hera: she is the goddess of the city. I think this underlines the importance of the role of the city as an intermediary to the gods: within the ideal circumstances, the city provides a frame of approach to the deities that assures their support and makes their distance more comprehensible. The mediation of the city allows the gods to show up benevolently. However, when the city does not provide the ideal conditions, the gods are rendered inaccessible and incomprehensible at best and punitive and vindicative at worst. This distinction between an ideal and a problematic city framework is very similar to the movement at the end of *Eumenides* where the chaotic dark punitive figures are turned into benevolent deities and integrated into the city. There is a break with the Homeric gods in that the relationship is not made any more between the individual and the god but through the city, and this new form of approach represents the difference between the chaos and the new order.

A new creed?

οἴμοι: πάρεργα (...) τάδ' ἔστ' ἐμῶν κακῶν,
ἐγὼ δὲ τοὺς θεοὺς οὔτε λέκτρ' ἃ μὴ θέμις
στέργειν νομίζω δεσμά τ' ἐξάπτειν χεροῖν
οὔτ' ἠξίωσα πώποτ' οὔτε πείσομαι,
οὐδ' ἄλλον ἄλλου δεσπότην πεφυκέναι.
δεῖται γὰρ ὁ θεός, εἴπερ ἔστ' ὀρθῶς θεός,
οὐδενός: ἀοιδῶν οἵδε δύστηνοι λόγοι.

1340-6

(Alas, this is an accessory to my troubles,
I do not think the gods fall prey to illegitimate love, or have their hands
   bond by each other,
I do not believe and will not be persuaded

> that they become tyrants over one another.
> Since a god, if he is properly a god,
> lacks nothing: these are the unfortunate stories of poets.)

These verses have been seen as the most problematic ones of this play. Is the theatrical illusion broken and the audience told that they are watching nothing more than lies? Because, indeed, what they would be watching are the lies of poets. It would be useful at this stage to give a brief review of the main positions in this matter.

Burnett argues that the action of Hera has nothing to do with petty conjugal motives but with a wrath proper to the gods. She argues that the word used by the messenger of the goddess (χόλος, wrath, 840), has nothing whatsoever to do with jealousy: 'This is the magnificent, almost personified wrath that sometimes came upon a Homeric warrior from outside himself' (1971: 176).

This interpretation is consistent with what we have seen about the representation of the hero and the gods in the first part of the play as essentially Homeric. This would mean basically that the claim of Heracles is in fact true: the cholera of the goddess does not come from jealousy or pure revenge, it comes from a right to be angry, of the kind found in Homeric gods, even if the motivations are not fully understood. Griffiths, on the other hand, suggests that Euripides might have had the intention to upset his audience with the 'lack of closure' (2006: 97).

The biggest problem with this interpretation is that I think there is no lack of closure in the play. The closure is there, and, in fact, we have a positive ending and the redemption of Heracles. I argue that there *is* a sense that something is wrong, but what is wrong is the way the aristocratic hero lacks the capacity to be integrated into the family and the polis. And for that the play offers a clear answer.

Kamerbeek suggests that *Heracles* does not deny the existence of the evil gods, it just denies them the status as gods (1966: 9). Michelini, on the other hand, reads the outburst as a break in the mimetic reality of the play: in the context of the play, what Heracles says is not true. We see gods committing crimes, and they are far from perfect beings that need nothing. But for the author, no play exists only at the level of mimesis, they are self-referential: 'At every point this play, of all Euripidean plays, has raised the question of the trustworthiness of poetic fiction' (Michelini 1987: 75).

Yunis (1988), on the contrary, believes this outburst is the main reason for the play – to propose a new creed:

> To sum up, I would expound 1340–1346 as follows: 'These examples of yours, Theseus, are irrelevant to my problems. For gods [in the sense which I shall specify in a moment] do not, as I view the matter, indulge in illicit love affairs and use handcuffs, nor have I ever viewed it otherwise nor will I, and the same holds for the notion that one is the master of another. My view depends on the strict sense which I am distinguishing [and in this case consists of] as the truly proper sense of the term god: in this strict sense god is the sort of being that lacks nothing. The examples [of the behavior of so-called gods] which you drew from the poets are tales of wretchedness.'
>
> 1988: 160–1

As we can see from these references, there is a tendency to review this outburst too much in the light of modern concepts. For example, Conacher states that Euripides time and again tried to show that: 'Greek myth, literally understood, presented a conception of the gods which was unworthy of belief by a civilized people' (1967: 38). However, myth was fundamental in Greek culture, religion and politics. The fact was that there was no stable creed in Greek religion.[8] The myths were fluid, adaptable and constantly subjected to new interpretations, yet they made up the core of Greek culture and permeated every aspect of everyday life. That, of course, does not exempt them from criticism. And we have plenty of evidence for criticism,[9] but I think that, as in this case, it is important to understand the criticism within its context. And the context of this play is quite clear: there are two sets of gods, the old Homeric way of understanding the gods, represented by Hera and by the absent Zeus, and the new face of the gods as within the polis, represented by Athena. Papadopoulou expresses a view that does not imply the rejection of gods, 'Although he does not deny the existence of the traditional gods, he rebels against them' (2005: 116). I agree with this view, however I think this rejection can be seen within the rejection of the old paradigm of the hero regulated by chaotic gods and the acceptance of the new polis religion.

This review of the literature makes it clear that the interpretation of divine behaviour in this play is problematic, however the answers seem to multiply and rarely converge to a unique satisfactory reading. Before attempting to give an answer, it is necessary to analyse the role justice has in this play and to compare it with Aeschylus' *Oresteia*, which will be the focus of the following sections.

Justice

The topic of justice is quite close to that of the gods and the madness: is there any justice in Heracles' madness? Indeed, the word δίκη (justice) is used to justify Hera's decision:

ἢ θεοὶ μὲν οὐδαμοῦ,
τὰ θνητὰ δ' ἔσται μεγάλα, μὴ δόντος δίκην

841–2

the gods will be nothing
and the humans will be mighty if justice is not served.

There has been a considerable amount of debate on the question of justice and its relation with the gods. Silk claims that the traditional motive for Hera's wrath, the jealousy for the fact that Heracles is the son of Zeus with Alcmena, is 'too remote from the play itself to be persuasive, and it is certainly nowhere mentioned in the text' (1985: 17–18). Looking at the text, the only explanation available is that of the verses quoted before: if Heracles does not pay the penalty, gods will be nothing and humankind (τὰ θνητὰ) will prevail. Heracles does not belong anywhere, he is more than a human and less than a god, therefore his own existence is a menace to the established order of the universe. It is a menace both to the gods and to men. This reading is certainly in conformity with the text.

And to add to this, Heracles' role as he appears in the play should have been just to save his family, not to seek vengeance. Once people were consecrated as suppliants to Zeus, it is Zeus' responsibility that the perpetrators should be punished.[10] But in the play, not only does the supplicant plot become merged with a revenge plot, Zeus and Heracles are merged, too. When seeing Heracles, Amphitryon claims, 'He is as good to save you as Zeus himself,' and Heracles not only takes upon him the role of saving his family, but he also takes the role of punishing those who threatened the suppliants. Within the plot, Heracles does indeed take the role that would have been expected of Zeus. The line between man and god disappears, Heracles is simultaneously both. Therefore, the killing of Lycus might have sounded quite strange to the audience, as it diverges from the traditional suppliant plot.[11]

Foley, too, points out that Heracles' madness has something to do with perverted rituals. Rituals are fundamental to the conduct of Greek public life: they function to unite men in a community, to define man's relation to the gods, and to control and contain violence internal to a community. However, Heracles has by his previous actions and by his very nature perverted these boundaries between men and gods, between individual and community. The children, who are at first described as a chorus attending the ritual of purification, turn into the sacrificial victims.

Papadopoulou also sees the relations between ritual and madness, even if she does not acknowledge the potential problems with the death of Lycus, for her the importance of this ritual for the madness of the hero is more significant because of the fact that, due to the righteousness of Lycus' killing, the purification would not be a requirement (2005: 18).

I will argue that the question is more nuanced. The comparison with the trilogy that commemorates the Athenian way to deal with justice, Aeschylus' *Oresteia*, will, I believe, help us explore a more complex construction.

Heracles and the Oresteia: Athena as the champion of justice

The central theme of the Oresteia is the transformation of old revenge justice into the justice of the city. That has been acknowledged many times before.[12]

We have seen how isonomy and the application of justice is one of the main themes of Athenian ideology. We have also seen this ideology is represented, for example, in the Stoa Poikile, where the Athenians are represented as the epitome of justice in the capture of Troy. The Athenians see themselves as the trustees of *sophrosyne* since the Homeric world. Isonomy is one of the first topics in the Pericles' funeral speech and in Theseus' defence of the Athenian democracy in Euripides' *Supplices*.

In the *Oresteia*, we actually see this justice being created. The two first plays are dominated by *alastors* and miasmas that are extended from one generation into the other, until Orestes finds himself in the impossible position of either living up to this role as avenger of his father or sparing his mother's life. He has to choose between being persecuted by his father's spirit or his mother's Erinyes. As we know, he chooses his father and ends up being tormented by his mother's vengeful spirits. Violence and revenge, miasma and blood just ended up out of control. The solution found by Aeschylus is simply to move the problem to Athens and have it solved in a proper court. A court would, by its very nature, end the cycle of violence and revenge.

But what has *Heracles* to do with that trilogy? In the first place, in both plays the problem of justice is quite relevant. In the prologue of the play, we are told a story of blood and revenge that has been going on for generations (26–43). The details that Amphythrion tells the audience are an example of mythological obscurity, the stories are not well known and they underline an image of blood, revenge and fight for power that seems to just hang over and cloud the existence of Heracles' family. As well as that, during most of the play the references to justice are simply equal to revenge. Lycus wants to kill the children because he is afraid of justice, that is, he his afraid that the children will avenge their father (οὔκουν τραφέντων τῶνδε τιμωροὺς ἐμοὶ χρῄζω λιπέσθαι, τῶν δεδραμένων δίκην – For certainly, I do not need these once grown up into avengers, bringing justice for my deeds 168–9). This is the justice that prevails in Heracles' world. In the second place, both choruses are constituted by old male citizens of the city, and the references to their age and lack of power echoes the Aeschylian chorus.

What we have in both plays is a pollution that is extended for generations, a representation of the old order that needs to be substituted by a new order, the old world only has a solution in Athens.

And just as Athena and the Areopagus[13] forgive the guilt of Orestes, Theseus downplays the role of Heracles' *alastor* (οὐδεὶς ἀλάστωρ τοῖς φίλοις ἐκ τῶν φίλων no alastor passes on from friend to friend – 1234). In Athens, this old system prevails no more. In Athens, justice is a symbol of democracy and equality. The future is only safe in Athens with new altars and new rituals that safeguard the citizen as well as the city.

Within the context of this comparison, it is possible to reframe the question of justice. Even if we agree that there is a perversion of rituals and of the boundaries between men and gods, it is quite clear that the punishment is much too strong for the fault. But on this point, I must agree with Martha Nussbaum:

> Greek tragedy shows good people being ruined because of things that just happen to them, things that they do not control. This is certainly sad; but it is an ordinary fact of human life, and no one would deny that it happens. Nor does it threaten any of our deeply held beliefs about goodness, since goodness, plainly, can persist unscathed through a change of external fortunes.
>
> 1986: 25

It is sad, but it is a good way of reading the world. And, more important than that, in the outdated world of heroes, champions, blood and revenge, the chances of the punishment being completely out of proportion with the crime are highly multiplied. The new order offers solutions to avoid this: justice, courts, a written law system, equality, rituals that are meant to keep open the communication with the gods. There is a solution for the problem of this tragedy, but only in Athens. This is very well aligned with the Athenian and Athenian tribunal's role in the league of Delos.[14]

Having discussed the relevant literature on the topic and having drawn a parallel with Aeschylus, we are now in a position to revisit the questions stated at the beginning of the chapter: where is Zeus? Is Zeus at all reliable to save his family? What is the role of Hera in Heracles' madness? Why does Hera attack? Is it a plain vengeful act or is Heracles somehow deserving of such punishment by the gods?

Zeus is nowhere to be seen. In a first moment the audience might have thought that the return of Heracles was Zeus' answer to the suppliants' prayers, only to find out that his return means actually the end of their lives. In the first part of the play, we find the bitter words of Amphitryon against Zeus (343). These words will be negated by the chorus at 798–801, just after Heracles' revenge against Lycus. Yet, at the end of the play they will be picked up by Heracles, maybe even with greater bitterness, as Heracles completely rejects Zeus as a father and sees the god as the source of all his sufferings (1262–4).

There is no appearance of Zeus or an oracle that might enlighten us on his will. Even the goddesses that appear make no reference to him except to say he is the father of Heracles and the husband of Hera. Both tradition and the text imply that Hera's antagonism is motivated by her jealousy over her husband's actions. Therefore, in a way, the link between Heracles and the source of his madness is Zeus, but we have no clue about what is Zeus' opinion on what is going on. Zeus never acts, never speaks, never sends a messenger.

On the other hand, Hera sends two goddesses on stage, Iris and Lyssa, with the task of turning the hero mad. Nevertheless, despite having more than 50 verses spoken by these goddesses, we have but two that justify the madness, and those two are not at all clear in their meaning. Hera is simultaneously present and absent. She has a message and messengers with a job to do. We know she is responsible for the madness, but the goddess herself is not present. And the reasons for her action are left in deliberately vague terms. There is some notion of justice, but no notion of Heracles' – or anyone else's – guilt.

We have seen that the idea of justice is a very important topic in Athenian ideology. In the *Oresteia*, we find a clear distinction between the old justice of revenge and murder and the new justice of courts and juries. These two kinds of justice are connected with different gods, the Erinyes on one hand (that go along with all the references to Zeus, who, once more, remains distant) and then Athena as the representation of this new justice. In the middle we find the Delphic Apollo, who clearly sides with Athena in the question of Orestes' guilt but is obviously impotent to solve the situation by himself.

In Euripides' play, Apollo is completely taken out of the equation, and we know that the myth normally attributed the labours as a punishment given by the Oracle of Delphi after the children's murder. Aeschylus brings a problem from Delphi to be solved in Athens, Euripides just ignores Delphi and changes the myth in order to be able to go straight to Athens.

We are left with two important goddesses in the play: the almost absent Hera and the very present Athena. Athena acts directly in the play, and her action prevents the catastrophic fulfilment of Heracles' madness by preventing the murder of his father. These are not two random goddesses: they are associated with two important cities in the ancient world, Hera is the patron of Sparta, and Athena, at least to the Athenians, of Athens. Here we have no gods of old versus new gods as we do in the *Eumenides*, both the goddesses are Olympian and 'new'. However, Athena's actions clearly anticipate what her city will do for the hero. It is the Athena Promachos the audience is faced with. It is the Athena of Athens. In a play where the rituals are clearly disrespected and the relationship between men and divinities seem turbulent and problematic, it is possible to find a clear distinction between religion inside and outside of

Athens. There is no religion in Greece that is not mediated by the polis, and the polis is fundamental to access the gods. In a city like Thebes all these relationships are perverted, and the gods seem clearly irrational, but so are the humans. It is the right city that provides the right way of accessing the gods, the right rituals, the right purification and ultimately the right way for the hero to be transformed into a worshipped cult hero and a god. Outside Athens there is chaos, even for the gods.

Heracles in Athens: The chorus

The analysis of the role of the gods in the previous sections implies an opposition between Athens and Thebes. This opposition is further highlighted by the construction of the chorus, who represent Thebes and the Thebans. Therefore, the relationship of the chorus with the hero represents the relationship between Thebes and Heracles. A close look at these odes and at the relationship the chorus develops with the main characters will add another layer to this opposition.

The chorus of Heracles, composed by old Thebans (very old as they keep reminding us), is very aware of itself as a chorus. The odes are filled with references to singing and dancing, they introduce themselves as ἀοι-|δὸς ὥστε πολιὸς ὄρνις (grey-haired bards like the grey swan, 110–11). The references to music and dance are multiple in these odes[15] and the chorus is very aware of their function, but they do not seem to find the right kind of song to sing.[16] We have references to hymn, peaen and lament, but what song does the chorus in fact sing?

At a first look, we would expect lament. That is indeed what is first suggested by the swan metaphor, and that is what the chorus keeps saying.[17] After all, lament is the most appropriate song to what is happening on stage. Heracles went to Hades, and apparently he is dead. Lycus is ready to murder all of Heracles' family: father, wife and children. Yet, there is not much lament in these odes. The thing the chorus laments the most is, actually, the fact that they are too old to be able to help Heracles' family. They focus on Heracles' deeds and on their own incapacity to save his family – not exactly in lament. Even if we take a close look at the vocabulary, formal words for mourning like θρῆνος or γόος (lament and wailing) are much less frequent in this play than in other Euripidean plays, with three references in the entire play.[18]

As Swift (2010) notes, at the beginning of the first stasimon, they seem to have the need to justify which kind of song they are singing, so unexpected is their choice. Therefore, the threnic tones, even if mentioned, are not much exploited. This chorus is not a chorus of mourners.

It has been noted that these songs have echoes from hymn and popular song. Bond (1981: 91–4), for example, points out that the length and structure of the first stasimon (three pairs of stanzas with a three-line coda or refrain after each stanza, three being a sacred number) as well as the metres (aeolic) are associated with cult songs. Adding to the form, the mention of the divine birth of the hero, the praise given to him and his description as saviour and protector does bring strong cultic tones, somehow echoing what is promised to the hero by Theseus at the end of the play: his everlasting cult in Athens.

Apart from the hymnic interferences, it has been clearly demonstrated that these songs owe a lot to epinician.[19] Parry in 1965 argued that the epinician topics in the second stasimon helped make sense of this song in the play. Swift (2010) developed this idea and emphasized the importance of these tones in all the odes. But while Heracles is usually presented in epinicians in a favourable light as a semi-god, in this play it is his humanity that is salient, not so much his divinity. Swift, therefore, binds the choral odes into one aristocratic ode to an athlete, which is ultimately dismissed in the last words of Heracles when he says that friendship and not any athletic success or wealth is the highest good.

Yet, these odes still present some problems. First, is the very composition of the chorus. Choruses are normally somehow linked to one of the main characters of the play. Therefore, we would expect companions of Heracles or maybe women attending Megara. But this is a chorus of old Thebans, old companions in arms of Amphitryon, not Heracles. It is true that they sing about the hero, but they seem to have no real connection with him.

Another rather strange thing is that the third stasimon ends at 814, just as Lyssa appears on the roof of the palace. For the next more than 600 lines there is no choral ode for the chorus. Why does the chorus cease acting like a chorus right in the middle of the play? Of course, the chorus is on stage until the very end; actually, theirs are the very last words of the play, as usual. They engage in dialogue with the characters, they even sing a song, some kind of monody with no strophic responsion. They are there, they just stop behaving like a chorus.

To explain this, I would like to go back to the first stasimon (strophe A). I would like to focus my attention for a while on the word εὐλογία. Even if this word appears a couple of times in epinician literature, this is the only occurrence in all extant tragedy. It is not a tragic word. Actually, I would like to argue that this is a political word. In fact, this is the very word used by Pericles in Thucydides to describe his funeral speech (Thuc. 2.42.1).

The importance of funeral speeches in Athens and their links with Athenian ideology has been clearly shown by Nicole Loraux (2006). Ziolkowski (1981) proposes a typology for the funeral speeches based on the extant examples. He identifies three main sections: *Proemium*, *Epainos* and *Paramythia*. In the first are normally announced the state burial, the impossibility of the task and the virtue of the dead. The epainos includes themes like γένος (kin), πατρίς (fatherland), ἔργα (deeds), i.e. the importance of filiation and belonging and the deeds of the dead. It also includes the following commonplaces: the dead benefitted their country and were noble and glorious, they possessed ἀρετή (excellence), fought with few against many, endured dangers, kept up the noble tradition, were autochthonous. Athenians are μόνοι (unique) in doing things, are superior to other Greeks, Athenians are superior in war, are superior on land and sea. The dead are famous, their fame is immortal, poets exalt the deeds of these men, they are deserving of our praise. Finally, the paramythia or consolation includes the topics: parents of the dead gained honour from their death, the dead get a state burial, the state provides for the children of the dead.

Of course, we cannot find every topic in these odes, yet it is worth having a close look at them. Some of the topics usually attributed to Athens are here attributed to Heracles.

The main topics of the ἔπαινος (praise) are γένος (kin), πατρίς (fatherland) and πρᾶξις (activity). We have plenty of references to the noble origin of the hero, even the use of the word εὐγενία, much used in the funeral speeches. We have one stasimon dedicated to his πρᾶξις, that is the famous twelve labours. However, the πατρίς, the connection within the city, is completely absent.

It has been noted that the twelve labours chosen are different from the ones represented in the Olympian metopes.[20] At least some Athenians would know these metopes, either by seeing them or by description. Of course, the canon of the labours was not fixed until much later. But the choice of the labours told in this ode is not accidental. In fact, from the six Peloponesian labours in Olympia, the chorus only refers to three. Heracles is chosen to be represented much less as a Peloponnesian hero, but as a Panhellenic champion. As we have seen, he even assumes some of the Athenian characteristics.

I would say this is why the chorus is mainly linked with Amphitryon. Amphitryon may be from Thebes, the Heracleidai might be Peloponnesians, but Heracles is much more than that, as all his links with Thebes are somehow neglected in this play.

Going back to the funeral speech structure, these odes miss one of the big parts: the *consolatio*. There is no consolation anywhere. And we would really expect it. In funeral speeches, a great deal of consolation derives from the fact that the dead died for the good of their city, and the state, therefore, gives them a public burial and assumes the responsibilities for the protection and education of the orphans. If we look at the odes from this perspective, the lack of consolation is even more pungent and tragic. Here in Thebes, different to Athens, not only does the hero, despite all the goodness he brought to humankind, lacks a proper burial, his children, instead of protected are threatened with death.

In drama, Thebes is, as Zeitlin (1990) suggested, an inverse image of Athens, an anti-Athens, a city where all Athenian characteristics are absent. And here the lack of structure, the lack of community support is particularly striking. What in Athens belongs to the citizens, here belongs to the individual. And whilst in a citizenship structure each individual relies on the community, here the community is useless.

These odes also echo the choral odes from Aeschylus' *Agamemnon*, the use of the word αἴλινον in verse 348, quite a rare word in ancient tragedy, seems to recall the chorus of *Agamemnon* (αἴλινον αἴλινον εἰπέ, τὸ δ' εὖ νικάτω – we say a lament, a lament, but may the good prevail – Aeschylus, *Ag.* 121). We have seen the importance of connections with the *Oresteia* in this play. But different to the chorus of Erinies in *Eumenides* who end up accepting Athenian salvation, this chorus, made up of old men as in *Agamemnon*, remains in Thebes, remains in the revenge world. It is quite interesting that it is the chorus in the third stasimon that narrates the death of Lycus. Normally, these kinds of events are described by a messenger, just as it will be a messenger that will describe the murder of the children, yet the chorus takes upon itself the task of narrating and rejoicing in the revenge.

The chorus stops being a chorus because they have no more to sing as a chorus: they can sing of great victories, they can sing of revenge, to sum up they can sing about the great deeds of a hero, but they cannot support him, they cannot offer any consolation, and once the climax happens and Heracles kills his own children, it is not in their hands to give any support or redemption. What the chorus lacks will be introduced on stage by Theseus. The last two lines of the play are particularly striking:

> στείχομεν οἰκτροὶ καὶ πολύκλαυτοι,
> τὰ μέγιστα φίλων ὀλέσαντες.
>
> 1427-8
>
> we go now, pitied and much lamented,
> having lost our biggest friend.

How does the chorus lose his friend? Amphitryon is alive, Heracles is safe. What is the sense of ὀλέσαντες? Amazingly enough, none of the commentaries on this play says much about these lines. They are just regarded as the mark of the exodus of the chorus. Yet, they are quite puzzling. They reflect, I think, the relationship between Heracles and Thebes. The chorus had stated that they never want to lose their garland, yet Theseus says that Heracles will be the garland of Greece, through his role and worship in Athens (1331-5).

The function of the chorus as a chorus is over, the praises to Heracles will be sung no more by Thebes but by Athens. This chorus can only sing the glory of the aristocratic hero in an epinician manner. They can rejoice in the ancient world of great heroes and revenge, but not in the new world of community and justice. These old Theban men lack the community support needed to deliver a *consolatio*, needed to deliver a proper funeral speech. They want to sing a eulogy, but they keep drifting from it.[21] And when Heracles refuses the glory of the aristocratic victor in favour of friendship and a community in which to be integrated, these men are left with nothing but lamentation.

The message of *Heracles* is clear: you can be a hero anywhere, but it is only worth being so if you are in Athens, where true friendship, i.e. allyship, resides. But these men from Thebes stay outside Athens. They lose even the little they had, the song in honour of the victor, because that garland belongs now to Athens. There is neither salvation nor a future for them.

A tale of two cities: Athens vs Thebes

That the play is set in the city of Oedipus is not absolutely necessary since the hero had connections with many cities, it is a choice of the poet. It is important to make clear that Thebes in the Athenian dramatic stage is not exactly the city situated more or less 80 kilometres from Athens, it is a literary construction. As we have seen, Zeitlin (1990) has argued that, out of all the mythic spaces, Thebes is the most tragic. It is the city of Oedipus, one of the most important tragic cycles. But the whole story of the city is filled with tragic material, since the killing of Ares' dragon. The story of the city is a story of excess, self-centredness and perverse fertility: the earth itself gives birth to their first inhabitants, but they end up killing each other, a mother gives birth to the sons of her own son. Thebes is the place where there is no redemption, no future, there are survivors but never descendants: Agave outlives Pentheus, Oedipus outlives Eteocles and Polynices, Creon outlives Haemon and Menoeceus, Heracles kills his own children.

Therefore, this is the perfect space to be used as an antithesis of Athens; tyranny versus democracy, chaos versus order, exclusion instead of inclusion.[22] This is contrary to Athens, which is in tragedy always the space for redemption, as we can see in Aeschylus' *Eumenides*, Sophocles' *Oedipus Coloneus* and Euripides' *Supplices* and *Heraclidae*.

Thebes is not the necessarily the place for Heracles, but the role of Thebes and its anti-democratic patterns is very important for the play. The choice of Thebes as the space for the madness allows for the deepening of the difference between this space and Athens.

Athens is in tragedy the place for salvation.[23] On the other hand, it is not just that Thebes is the city of chaos. Thebes is actually used on stage to represent the opposite of Athens and therefore underline the image of this city. It is curious that the myth of foundation of Thebes and Athens both involve autochthony: the Spartoi and Erecthonius, and this is reflected in the play in the first reference to each city (cf. 4–8 and 1163–71, respectively).

Images of autochthony did not make the Athenians unique in Greece, but it set them apart from the Dorian Peloponnesians, who were said to descend from the Heraclidae.[24] The big difference is that in the first case, that autochthony is stained by blood and murder. The Spartoi are violent creatures that have to be annihilated. And more than blood and murder is the murder of one's own, as they in fact kill one another. It is the germ of civil war, of chaotic violent revengeful war, living up to their role as descendent from Ares. In Athens, on the other hand, the autochthony just gives origin to life. And Athens is represented time and again as the place of redemption for the chaotic Theban cycles, for example in Euripides' *Heraclidae* Athens provides refuge to the hounded and displaced children of Heracles, in Euripides' *Supplices* Theseus leads an army to recover the corpses of the Argive army killed in the war between Eteocles and Polinices and, finally, in the Sophocles *Oedipus Coloneus* it is Athens that provides shelter for Oedipus in his final hour.[25]

It is very important to note the role given to Athens in terms of politics and cult in redeeming Oedipus of his curse, because, as we will see, these are the same devices that are used in Euripides' play to redeem Heracles.

Thebes is the space of blood and murder, the space of rivers of tears.[26] Thebes is the continuation of the space of the labours. Indeed Heracles refers to the killing of his children as his last labour. In Thebes, Heracles is not home yet, he is still in the world of strife, of monsters, the space where he has to be the violent champion, the vengeful aristocrat. Only in Athens can Heracles be truly human.

Rehm also notes that in the play, Thebes is a perverted space in terms of ritual and expectations.[27] Megara, even before the appearance of Heracles, in dealing with the children confuses sacrificial, nuptial and burial rites (467–85).

Later, being attacked by their own father, the children run to what Rehm calls 'the symbolic cornerstones of Greek domestic life: mother, house, gods', but none offers real refuge. Their death is in fact a parody of their future expectations. The first son was promised the palace of Eurystheus and he himself is killed against the pillar of the same palace. The second son who was promised rule over Thebes, and who used to play with his father's club, sees his death coming by means of the very same club at the altar of his Theban home. Finally, the third son, the one who was promised Oechalia, the city conquered with the bow, encounters death, together with his mother, by means of an arrow of that same bow. 'Each son gains a shadow image of his inheritance, his future home reduced to a deadly interior of the palace' (Rehm 2002: 107).

It has also been noted that there is an inversion of the suppliant model in this play. The suppliant theme is fairly usual in tragedy, where a group of people takes hold of a sacred space and trusts in the gods to deliver them. The sacred space in itself is the only protection a suppliant has.[28] However, the attitude of Megara in this play is quite different to this: 'A true suppliant is passive; he moves only when he is forced (...) Megara on the other hand, abandons her altar of her own free will' (Burnett 1971: 162).

In addition, Burnett (ibid.), for example, shows how the play exposes a series of perversions of traditional rituals that would make the audience feel, at least, uncomfortable. One of his main points has to do with the way in which the suppliant theme, that we find at the beginning of the play, is persistently perverted: what seems like a regular suppliant situation where we expect the traditional outcomes – violence, force, death – turns into exactly the opposite, frustrating the expectations in such circumstances, that is, to see the suppliants 'easily agree to leave their sanctuary' (p. 159).

Leaving sanctuary is one of the standard motives of suppliant drama, and there is always an attempt to make the suppliants move, which the suppliants refuse to do. Here, the argumentation in order to leave sanctuary comes from one of the suppliants: Megara. Lycus has not much to do in his role, and Megara, despite being at the altar of Zeus, does not show any faith whatsoever in the god, she abandoned all hope and is ready to face death, her death and that of her children. I agree with Burnett that, even if the nuances of the suppliant drama are slightly difficult to feel in our contemporary world, they would have been perceptible enough for an audience very much used to not only this kind of drama, but also to the historical reality of the suppliant role.

As we have seen before, Heracles behaviour is also out of place.[29] Both Megara and Heracles somehow disrespect what is seen as the appropriate attitude towards the gods. Megara tries to solve her problem and that of her children by her own hands, instead of waiting for the divine intervention she sought as a suppliant and Heracles acts in place of Zeus as the avenger of those who were violent against the gods' suppliants. The fact is that the suppliants, with the exception of Amphitryon end up dead, not at the hands of their enemy, but at the hands of their supposed saviour. The inversion of ritual seems to have the most tragic consequences.

Athens to the rescue

All this question of strife brings us to the end of the play, the third part, after Heracles has killed his children. This final part has often been regarded as an almost meaningless coda, yet I think the sense of the play depends on the reading of this last part. Here the hero finally finds his salvation, but for that he has to withstand a deep transformation, and this transformation is deeply linked with Athens. We have seen that Heracles is the hero of all excess. Here in the last scenes of the play, the hero has to stop being *that* hero. He has to assume his humanity in order to be integrated into Athens. From now on he belongs to a city, to a community. And it is only when the hero is completely stripped of his divinity that he opens the path to become a god with proper cult as such in Athens. The hero only becomes a true hero when he starts acting for the benefit of the community.

Burnett had already noted this last movement of salvation, where Theseus plays the role of champion: 'the last drama of the Heracles is formally a rescue action in which a desolate hero is found by his champion in a place of death and removed by him to a place of life' (1971: 173). But Theseus is more than a champion, he is the king of Athens and this redemption is closely linked to the city.

This salvation also means a reshaping of the hero. The hope in the divinity is not abandoned: as we have seen, the role of Athena is absolutely fundamental in the play. But this is the goddess of the city, and to belong to the city the hero has to adapt his heroic values and strength so that they benefit the city and not the individual. As Gregory suggests, the nature of Heracles as εὐγενής is fundamental throughout the play, but the ending scenes show an evolution of the concept from the aristocratic outlook of 'on individual glory and solitary accomplishment' (1991: 148–9). By accepting Theseus as a helper and Athens as a home, Heracles' notion of *eugenia* is transformed: 'he seems to affirm that one cannot do better than to live as an Athenian' (p. 149). His status is not dependent on his social standing or his deeds, but on his belonging to a community.

The end of Heracles, his redemption, his integration in Athens are a hymn to the city, to her power and her openness to accept whoever came to her, as long, of course, as her rules were accepted. To be an Athenian, Heracles has to change. Silk, too, underlines the transformation the hero has to go through:

> He sees himself opposed to the gods against whom men are helpless (1243, 1253), and so, as Theseus says, like an 'ordinary man' (1248), he proposes to die. (…) Theseus tempts him back to life with an offer of filia and a new home in Athens, where Heracles will be honoured in stone memorials and sacrifices after his death (1323–35). The honour is a hero's honour and presupposes Heracles' heroic past, but what is stressed is his death, stressed by a double formula: 'when you die, when you go to Hades' (1331). Euripides, therefore, does what Sophocles had never done, and negates Heracles' apotheosis altogether.
>
> 1985: 15–16

I do not agree that Heracles' apotheosis is negated. Theseus is human and his previsions are made from a human point of view. He cannot know the glories that are reserved for the hero. He gives the hero all he has to give. But the audience knows those glories. In fact, more relevant to this point would be the reference Heracles makes in verse 613 to the Holy Mysteries of Eleusis, that he claims helped him return from the Hades. For a mostly Athenian audience that reference would clearly indicate the timeline of myth and reinforce beforehand the connection of this version of hero with Athens. The audience also knows all the places of cult where the hero is honoured in Attica. By promising the hero his honours, Theseus is actually, without knowing, opening the path for apotheosis.

Happy endings

Despite all the misery that Heracles has to endure, the end of the play is actually a happy one. This, however, is not a universal opinion. Dunn (1996) has argued that the ending of *Heracles* is empty and meaningless:

> If Heracles will come to Athens, Theseus will give him gifts and land, and will see that his friend is honored by the city as a whole. And how will this

elusive sequel be honored? Not with a name or institution familiar to the audience, but with sacrifices and monuments that cannot be placed securely.

1996: 118

I would like to disagree on a few points. As we have seen in Chapters 3 and 4, the references to Heracles in Athenian architecture as well as the well-spread cult of the hero, would have been too obvious to ignore. The audience would think of them immediately: they were part of their everyday life. More than that, it actually gives a motive why Heracles has a much more important and widespread cult than the city's hero Theseus.

Furthermore, Dunn argues that the figure of Theseus is weak:

> Theseus has no official political authority. In this play he comes to Heracles not as ambassador of the city, but simply as a kinsman and friend (...) if Theseus is doubly deficient, then so too is the play: it lacks the presence of a *deus ex machina* who can resolve the action on stage before our eyes, and it lacks the presence of a civic ambassador who can guarantee a belated ending once the hero reaches Athens.
>
> 1996: 121–2

Theseus is clearly an ambassador and clearly an ally: Theseus is by default the King of Athens and he comes to Thebes as leader of an army. I do not think that this authority is at any point refused or even questioned. The arguments between Heracles and Theseus are the reshaping of Heracles' beliefs, a reshaping which is much needed if he is to continue with his life. And as to the emptiness of the offerings given to Heracles, I think that for the audience they would be anything but empty. Those shrines were indeed all over the city.

The reconstruction of the audience's cultural surface can thus contribute towards understanding the true meaning of this ending. If not universal, this reading of the end of the play is not unique either and it has been accepted in some recent studies. For example, Papadopoulou, too, sees the end of the play as a tale of redemption and happy endings where Athens and Heracles are glorified.[30] It is important to understand that Heracles was part of the everyday life of the audience. The sanctuaries of the hero were all over Attica. As Rehm points out, some were even visible from the theatre: Kynossarges, one of the most important sanctuaries in Attica was visible to those sitting in the higher rows of the theatre.[31] This surface was sufficiently established not to be missed by the audience.

Friendship and salvation are fundamental in this play, and yes, as one by one all the answers fail, the Thebans, Greece, Zeus, Heracles, the ultimate answer comes in the form of Athena, Theseus and, therefore, Athens.

The previous analysis clearly demonstrated that the play is built on the opposition between Thebes and Athens, Thebes fails time after time to give the hero what only Athens can give: friendship, salvation, glory, honour, even a funeral speech or some consolation. Thebes, represented mainly by the chorus, is useless to Heracles and his family, and therefore they end up losing the hero. The happy ending is just for those who are able to go thought the changes that will ultimately lead them out of the old chaotic world and into the new luminous world of democratic Athens and her ἀρχή (sovereignty).[32]

7

Conclusion

ἥκω (...), σῷ παιδί, πρέσβυ, σύμμαχον φέρων δόρυ.

(I have come, (...) old man, bringing your son the spear of an ally.)

Eur., *Her.* 1163–5

After the death of Pericles in 429, Athens is left with a vacuum of power. New names appear on the political scene, names of aristocrats with different opinions and different policies but normally with a strong thirst for power and personal glory: Cleon, Nicias, Alcibiades. At the same time, Sparta was offering support to any allies who would want to rebel against Athenian ἀρχή, therefore questioning the leadership of Athens, especially after the number of men dropped significantly with the plague:

> Thucydides' last reported speech of Pericles in book 2 depicts the dynamic Athenian leader encouraging the people of Athens to be patient and maintain their naval empire. Above all Pericles warned against expanding the empire while at war. This plan might well have worked, had the Athenians stuck to it. But Thucydides' narrative clearly states that after Pericles' death the Athenians did just the opposite: eventually private ambition and the desire for honor and wealth won out over the interests of the city.
>
> Evans 1992: 131

When in 417, during the celebration of the new temple to Apollo in Delos, Nicias took his private money to build a temporary floating bridge between Delos and Rheneia,[1] and in the following year Alcibiades decided to sponsor no less than seven chariot teams at the Olympic games,[2] one of the biggest democratic fears was just turning into reality before Athenian eyes: individual thirst for power and glory was taking the place of the welfare of the community.

It is in this very context that Euripides writes his *Heracles*.[3] The threat of individuals radiating their glory that is seen as greater than the city's and using it for their own purposes was as real as it had been seventy years earlier when Athens used Heracles in the treasury at Delphi to warn about the dangers of aristocratic power. At the same time, Athens needed more than ever to reinforce her position in the empire.

How, then, does the play fit into this context? One of the most striking features in the play is the total change in the order of myth. As far as we can tell, before Euripides, the labours were the punishment Heracles had to endure after killing his children, the punishment given to him when he sought purification at Delphi. By changing the myth, Euripides reinforces a series of questions that are particularly relevant to the Athenian context.

In the first place, this version implies that Delphi, which normally has a significant importance for the myth of Heracles, is completely eradicated from the myth in favour of an all-Athenian purification.

Besides, this version of the myth gives Theseus the upper hand, while traditionally it is Theseus who owes Heracles for being saved from Hades, or at least underlines reciprocity and the importance of friendship and alliances.

This also makes it possible to trace a clear line between the life of Heracles before and after Athens. Before, we have the aristocratic, violent, chaotic hero, brave – certainly – civilizing even, but whose excess culminates in the killing of his own family.

And finally, by killing his own children immediately before going to Athens, and by saying to Theseus that he is now his child, Euripides eliminates the existence of the Heraclidae (it is interesting to note that the term never appears in this play and that the children are always referred to as children of Heracles, never of Heraclidae). If we bear in mind that the Spartan kings claimed to be descendants of the Heraclidae, Heracles is transferring his heritage from Sparta and the Peloponese to Athens, along with his glory and his protection.

Heracles had an important presence in Athenian monumental and public buildings. These buildings had a significant role in creating or reinforcing an ideology, namely the role of Athens as city of salvation and his metamorphosis into the aristocratic hero that accepts the city and is accepted by her. They were present in the citizens' everyday life.[4]

In Athens, as we have seen, Heracles had a very important place in religion. The material existence of temples and cult places in itself represents a relationship between the city and the hero.[5] But in Heracles' case, there is an even bigger proximity: for he is at the same time both human and divine, because he aggregates around him those who do not really belong to the polis as full citizens and because most of his cults in Attica imply a communal meal:

> What the artists try to express here is the fact that, by feasting, Heracles does exist, very near his human fellows: he is not only the divinity who provides meat but also the god who dare participate in the human *deipnon*.
>
> Verbank-Piérard 1992: 105

There is a close, almost personal, relationship with the hero. I think this importance in cult had a significant role in assuring Heracles' figure shows up again and again, in different political contexts, in different situations and for different purposes, as the propaganda of Athens evolves.

The self-image of Athens is a very powerful one, where deed and literature, myth and history merge together to form a version of history that corresponds to the image the city has of itself.

Thucydides suggests Athens needs no Homer because her deeds are so great that they speak for themselves (2.41.4). It is true that Athens had no Homer, but it had a Thucydides, an Aeschylus, a Sophocles, an Euripides and in one way or another, they contributed to create that self-image, by recalling the Athenian deeds, by recalling time and again the myths that made the city what it was. They helped not only to create that image, but also to preserve it for us.

And to prove that those myths are absolutely fundamental in Athenian self-image, even Aristotle quotes the myth of the rescue of the Heraclidae alongside Marathon (Aristotle, *Rhet.* ii.22.1396a).

We have evidence that from the 440s, with the competition with Sparta and then during the Peloponnesian War, the way Athens deals with her allies becomes more and more strict. As we have seen, Athens is set to control the politics, economy and justice of her allies.[6] As these events happened, Athenian propaganda adapted to the circumstances.

This kind of control over the allied cities is, of course, supported by an ideology that justifies the Athenian leadership. The myth of Ion, namely alongside the Athenian hero Theseus, was fundamental to justify the Athenian position in the Aegeus; her position in the mainland, however, was much more complicated. From the beginning of the fifth century, most of the cities of the Peloponnese had a connection with Sparta. Not only that, but the Athenian military power was also clearly focused on her fleet, Athens even tries to turn herself into an island by creating a direct path between the city and her port. The connection with the Piraeus ensures that her control over the seas is not threatened. If it is true that much of Athenian attention was focused on the islands and Ionia, Attica itself was in the mainland, and Athens needed allies there. The relationship with Ion does not justify any claims in the mainland; Athens is forced to choose another hero who could be the image of her ideology. And that here is clearly Heracles. Heracles is well known, has connections with most cities in Greece and represents in Athens as the city wants to be perceived as, that is, the place open to receive whoever wants to stay there and the place that offers the best solutions to all kinds of problems. The connection of Heracles with the Eleusian mysteries is fundamental, not only to give this festival a Panhellenic status, but also to show this newly transformed hero, the hero who went to Hades and back, the hero who is made Athenian, the hero who represents the possibility of being welcomed both in Athens and in the other life.

At the same time, Heracles brings with him a powerful internal message for the Athenians. Heracles used to be the lonely, violent, aristocratic hero. The evolution we find both in the iconography and the literature of the fifth century is clearly evidence that Athens is exploring a new representation of the hero (and not only this hero, but other heroes, as, for example, we have seen in *Ajax*), and this representation is clearly connected with the city. The aristocratic hero is turned into the benevolent hero who brings glory to the city and her citizens. That is the point of being an aristocrat, that is the main point of being an aristocrat in a democracy.

We have seen that the play fully engages with some of the main topics of Athenian propaganda. We can find a campaign that aims to promote Athens as the leading city of the Greek world. Athens wants not only to preserve her ἀρχή in the League, but also to extend it as much as possible in answer to the Spartan attacks. So, Athens tries to promote herself as a source of the great gifts of the Greek civilization: the victory over the barbarians, law, justice, equality, democracy, even the act of ploughing the land, all come from Athens. At the same time, Athens tries to assure a united front within the city and fight her worst nemesis: the rise of aristocratic power. Heracles is a very important piece in this ideology, his initiation in the mysteries make him the ultimate example of the benefits given by Athens to all Greece, even non-Athenians. Heracles serves the purpose of representing an ideology of integration and salvation. That this was a very important topic and quite relevant for the Athenians, is indicated by the amount of Attic pottery we can find representing both Heracles in Eleusis and Heracles in the underworld.

By the end of the fifth century, the Athenian position becomes more and more compromised. Sparta is supporting any rebellion against her ἀρχή. The revolts start to multiply and to be crushed with increasing violence. At the same time, the plague left Athens with a huge gap in human resources and with a lack of leadership after the death of Pericles. The fights between powerful aristocrats to control the city and their different approaches to the Athenian military strategy leave the city even more fragile. Although the date for the play is not certain, it would be quite close to the Sicilian disaster, a moment when the city needed more than ever to broadcast her ideology.

There are several audiences for Athenian propaganda, and as we have seen, different myths provide answers to those audiences. As Ion is used in Ionia, Athens tries to use Heracles in the mainland. At the same time, Heracles was a powerful warning about the dangers of aristocrat power within the city itself. So, for the case of Heracles, I would like to propose the existence of two target audiences: the Greek cities, mainly those of the Peloponnese, and the aristocracy of Athens herself. To the Greek cities, Athens wants to show her openness and welcoming politics for those who want to be her allies, as well as all the benefits the city can provide. To the aristocrats in Athens, Heracles, namely Euripides' *Heracles*, represents a model of behaviour, the choice each and every aristocrat has to make: to be centred in their own interests and power and be lost or to share their glory (and their power and wealth) with the city and be welcomed, transformed and saved. Thus, the play is perfectly integrated with the cultural surface of the audience, both playing with its tensions and reinforcing the ideology of the audience.

One of the main characteristics of propaganda is the use of all or most of the methods available to promote a certain ideology. As far as we can tell, Athens uses all the techniques available: oratory, tragedy, religion, iconography.

Heracles is present and used in all of them, as we have seen. There is a special interest in placing the hero in Panhellenic spaces or moments, like Delphi or the Great Dionysia, in order to maximize the audience available and spread the propaganda more easily. As we can take from the case of Heracles, the use of propaganda was as global as possible, associating word, image and cult whenever attainable.

Once again, I would like to underline that the aim of this study is not to give a full image of Athenian propaganda, or to provide a linear and unique reading of Euripides' *Heracles*, but rather to look at one example of the articulation between propaganda and a cultural surface and how artistic works can, at the same time, play with the tensions on that surface and be a part of it. I also believe that the reading of Euripides' play within this model can bring forward aspects that would otherwise go unnoticed as well as make sense of some of the biggest problems normally attributed to the play. Reading the play within the context of Athenian ideology and propaganda does not at all change the meaning of the play or in any way make irrelevant any other readings, however it can help make sense of some otherwise obscure details.

It could be very interesting and potentially very enriching to apply this framework to more heroes as to their use in the city and tragedy. To analyse evidence from different source materials and different areas can help us take a much better picture of Athenian tragedy and Athenian ideology.

Having said all this, I think it is quite clear that for most people in the theatre of Dionysus that day, the name of Heracles would bring to mind the great Panhellenic hero who had a special role in Athens, the hero who was all over the city, the hero who helped the city to fight the Persians in Marathon, the hero of great communal meals, a hero who was a god, the hero who was too unique to fit into traditional categories and the one that was a constant warning against the dangers of aristocratic arrogance. But also, the hero who went to the underworld and came back, the hero who opened the path of the Eleusinian mysteries, the one who brought back the apples of the Hesperides. And I would say that all those thoughts were used and played with by Euripides.

Notes

Chapter 1

1. The allied cities brought their annual tribute to Athens during the Great Dionysia. For a detailed description of the rituals before and during the festival, see Pickard-Cambridge, Gould and Lewis ([1968] 1988) and Goldhill (1987).
2. For example, Arrowsmith, in the introduction to his translation of the play, states: 'The result is a structure in which two apparent autonomous actions are jammed savagely against each other in almost total contradiction, with no attempt to minimize or even to modulate the profound formal rift' in Grene and Lattimore (1959), 268.
3. To quote:

   > Despite the discussions of a hundred years, the unity of Euripides' Herakles remains a problem. Most scholars have distinguished in the play three parts whose limits are marked by the apparition of Lussa with Iris (814) and by Herakles' recovery from madness (1088) : but over the relationship of these three parts to each other and to the whole there has been little agreement.
   >
   > Bond 1981: xvii–xxvi

4. Cf. Sheppard (1916).
5. Cf. Foley (1985); Michelini (1987).
6. Conacher (1955), 82.
7. Cf., e.g. Barlow (1982), 116.
8. Burnett: 'An ultimate fourth action of divine salvation, one that will rescue him even from his remorse and set him banqueting among the gods, will soon be produced for Heracles, but of this he knows nothing at all' (1971: 180–2).
9. For a full discussion of the positions on this question, see Gregory (1977); and Papadopoulou (2005).
10. Goldhill (2000b), 67 ff.
11. Jauss (1982), 21.
12. Schmitz (2007), 160.
13. Ibid., 167.
14. Scott (2010).
15. Neer and Kurke (2019), 2.

16 Ibid., 4.
17 See Fischer-Lichte (2009, 2010).
18 Roland Barthes, with his *S/Z* in the beginning of the 1970s, introduced within a group of five codes that constituted the text (hermeneutic, semantic, proairetic, cultural and symbolic), the notion of 'cultural code' as the 'references to a science or a body of knowledge' (1974: 20), by collecting all the cultural codes available to a certain community, i.e., the general knowledge available to them, we find ideology (p. 97).
19 Barbato (2020), ix–x.
20 Griffin and Carter: 'The plays may not be tied closely to contemporary events and personages, but they do engage with the institutions, as well as the ideology, of the democracy' (2011: 10).
21 Kennedy: 'Tragedy is, in many ways, no different than a public monument or a democratic institution, such as the assembly, in the way it participates in the creation and maintenance of civic identity. The interpretative community, however, would be just as much a passive recipient of these identities as it would have been an active creator' (2009: 65).
22 Kennedy's argument, for example, based on the iconographic representation of the end of the Trojan War in Athens, namely in the Stoa Poikile, is that the Athenians would have had a certain perspective on the massacre of the city that underlined the difference between general Greek barbarism and Athenian sophrosyne. These examples show that bringing back the text to their original material culture can in many ways offer new and fresh readings that would have been available to most of the audience. For Athanassaki, see, e.g., 2010 and 2018.

Chapter 2

1 See, e.g., Goldhill (1987), Griffin (1998) and Goldhill (2000a).
2 In Goldhill (1999), 10, 25–6. As Goldhill states:

> Pericles' building programme is only one of the most prominent examples of the glorification of empire through stone (...). The Stoa Poikile constructed a programme of images of military success, military memorials, and political statues (...) and above all, the Acropolis as a site itself and in relation to the Agora, all created monuments and spaces which were meant to do things to the citizen. Athens indeed was a city of images (as it was a city of words), and the role of such exemplary representation in the formation of the ideals of citizenship cannot be ignored.
>
> 25–6

3 Cf. Wilson (2000).
4 For a full discussion on the importance of oral tradition in Classical Athens, see Nagy (1996) and Thomas (1989).
5 Goldhill: 'When the Athenian citizen speaks in the Assembly, exercises in the gymnasium, sings at the symposium, or courts a boy, each activity has its own regime of display and regulation; each activity forms an integral part of the exercise of citizenship' (1999: 1).
6 Pickard-Cambridge, Gould and Lewis ([1968] 1988), 58–9.
7 See Trendall and Webster (1971).
8 Mills (1997); Kennedy (2009).
9 Reprinted in 2000, see Sourvinou-Inwood (2000).
10 Cf., e.g., Sokolowski (1955): 47, where it is quite evident that the different roles of priests and assemblies; the first as the people with the skills to ask the god and interpret his answer and the latter as the one who takes the decision.
11 For a neat and complete summary of the critics, see Hansen and Nielsen (2004), 130–4.
12 For an articulation of the temple's construction, Pindar and the relationship between Athens and Delphi, see Athanassaki (2011).
13 For a full account of the episodes we know, see McCauley (1999).
14 Cf. Hdt. 1,66–8.
15 Cf. McCauley (1999), 96 ff.
16 Cf. ibid., 91; see also Ekroth (2009), 125:

> Several instances are recorded of a community acquiring bones in order to strengthen its political position relative to that of its neighbors. Such hero cults were clearly propagandistic, as when the bones of Orestes were acquired by Sparta. Transferrals of cults were facilitated by the fluidity of myth, which allowed for the adoption or elaboration of different versions of the hero's history.

17 On Harmodius and Aristogeiton, see Garland (1992), 94 ff. For references, see the Introduction.
18 Cf., e.g., the way Athenians dealt with the war dead. See Loraux (2006) for a full account on the importation of the funeral speeches on the construction of the Athenian image.
19 Shear (2011), 1, highlights that:

> Just before the Great Dionysia of 409 BC, all the Athenians assembled by tribe and by deme swore an oath: I shall kill both by word and by deed and by vote and by my own hand, if I can, anyone who overthrows the democracy at

Athens, and if anyone holds office after the democracy has been overthrown in the future, and if anyone set himself up to be tyrant or if anyone helps to set up a tyrant. And if anyone else kills him, I shall consider him to be pure before both the gods and *daimones* (or spirits) because he killed an enemy of the Athenians, and, after selling all the property of the dead man, I shall give half to the killer and I shall not withhold anything. If anyone dies killing or attempting to kill such a man, I shall give benefits both to him and to his children just as to Harmodios and Aristogeiton and their descendants.

20 Gruppo di Ricerca Sulla Propaganda Antica, see Sordi (1974, 1975, 1976).
21 Syme (1939), even if applied to Rome, was a seminal work in this area. See also Proietti (2015) for the concept of 'Intentional History'.
22 Hornblower 'Propaganda' in OCD3.
23 Lasswell in Jackall (1995), 13.
24 In fact, the title *Propaganda* is the English translation for what is a plural form in the original *Propagandes*. Ellul (1973).
25 Ellul (1973), 62–3.
26 Loraux (1994, 2000, 2006).
27 See 'Fragments of a Lexicon to the Acropolis', in ibid. (1994), 23–6.
28 For a systematic study of these *topoi*, see Ziolkowski (1981). That the importance of such ideas as a base for formation was not incidental but was considered fundamental is stated by Plato in *Rep* 414 d–e.
29 See Arendt (2004), 462–3.
30 Cf. Taylor (1991).
31 Cf. Calame (2003), 114.
32 For a study of the myths of the origins of Athens and their political importance, see Bremmer (1987).
33 Cf. Osborne (2010), 250.
34 This idea of the importance of autochthony has been fully developed by Loraux (2000).
35 Nilsson: 'myths belong to the inventory of a certain kind of oratory, intended to excite patriotic sentiments, the speeches delivered at the state funeral of those who had fallen in a war. They are composed according to a general pattern, surveying the glorious deeds of the Athenians' (1986: 85).
36 Kennedy: 'Around the same time, we also see references to the courts in decrees pertaining to Athens' allies in the ἀρχή. The Phaselis (*IG* I^3 10), Miletos (*IG* i^2 22), and Chalcis (*IG* i^2 39) decrees assign certain cases for the allies to Athenian jurisdiction. Athens was exporting her judicial system just as they exported their democracy' (2009: 22). For a full discussion of the Athenian Imperial Jurisdiction see Meiggs (1972), 200–33. That Justice is one of the main arguments given by the Athenian

envoys to Sparta in 432, according to Thuc. 1.77, is also very relevant for the perception the Athenians had of themselves and the image they wanted to display.
37 Boedeker (2009), 47; see also Chapter 3 here.
38 Plut., *Lac. Apophth.* 236b–c, see Boedeker (2009), 62.
39 See Loraux (2006).
40 Ober:

> Institutions are accepted as legitimate (or rejected as illegitimate) on basis of ideological dispositions. At the same time, however, people's experience of formal institutions is a *source* of ideology and can strengthen or undermine ideological commitments. (...) The ideological dispositions of persons who live out their lives as subjects of institutional authority are inevitably influenced by the experience of being subject to the authority of those institutions.
>
> 2008: 272

41 See Loraux (1994), 23ff.
42 Samons II (2007), 293.
43 Kallet:

> If these liturgies were not financially necessary, why did the demos embrace liturgies so enthusiastically that the prevalent attitude was 'the more spent the better', and why were liturgists willing to spend so lavishly? From the perspective of the demos, or state, extravagance drained individual wealth, easing the disparity between rich and poor, and benefiting the city. Pseudo-Xen brings out the point (typically cast in negative terms): 'In the case of choral performances, athletic contests, and the command of warships, the demos knows that the wealthy pay while the people are entertained and obey. Therefore the people justifiably take the money (of the rich) so that they have it and the rich become poorer. At the same time they are a way of the aristocracy to show its relevance and power and was not of little importance to politics.'
>
> 1998: 55

44 Henderson:

> While the Periclean democracy championed a public and egalitarian ideology, and kept the private and family worlds as much as possible out of sight, drama focused on households and individuals, who moreover were often sympathetically at odds with the collective polis or its leaders; comedy in particular could voice criticism and advice that was both topical and sharply partisan. And while the democracy prized, and indeed depended on, rationality, self-sufficiency, progress and novelty, drama in the name of the gods and tradition cast all these into question. But in the end, it is hard to imagine that Athenian drama could have flourished as it did under any other system.
>
> 2007: 191–2

45 Haubold (2000), 184–90.
46 Ibid., 161–3.
47 Barbato (2020), 93.
48 Allan and Kelly (2013), 96.
49 See Connor (1992).
50 Rutishauser (2012), 8.
51 Cf. Meiggs (1972), 47.
52 Thuc. 1.44.1; IG I². 71 = SEG x.86. 20; ML 87. 17. See Meiggs (1972), 45.
53 Rutishauser:

> Ports in the Delian League could have been under some sort of Athenian supervision, perhaps from the inception but definitely by mid-century. there were large numbers of Athenian magistrates in allied cities, who could ascertain the provenance and destination of various cargoes. The Megarian Decree of the 430s, for example, would probably have been enforced by such officials if it was in fact related to commerce. It may have been intended mainly to cut off Peloponnesian trade with the back sea region since Megara had ties with her colony Byzantion (Thuc. 1.67.4, 1.139.1, 1.144.2).
>
> 2012: 111

54 Cf. Raaflaub (1998), 17.
55 See Rutishauser (2012), 240.
56 See Rhodes (2010), 56:

> The 420s appears to be a time when the nature of the Delian league was transformed. The league was kept in existence, but no longer in order to fight an unending war against Persia. All the members were required to send offerings to the Panathenaea, as if they were colonies of Athens. Decisions were taken for the whole League by Athens, and it is likely that when the treasury was moved to Athens the meetings held at Delos were discontinued.

57 Kroll: 'We should appreciate the importance of Athenian silver coinage in the Athenian ἀρχή, as the common monetary instrument whose production, dissemination and use were not activities that favoured political over commercial power, or vice versa, but means that simultaneously strengthened Athens' wealth and supremacy in both domains' (2009: 196–205). On the demand of the Athenian silver coinage in Egypt and the Levant, see p. 205. Rutishauser defendsthe principal motivations as also being economical and not only ideological:

> Traditionally this decree is also being interpreted as a purely political act by the Athenians to extend their dominance over the allies, with no economic motivations whatsoever. Since many Greek stating in the Aegean and already ceased minting

> silver by the mid-fifth century, the argument continues that it was not Athenian mandate but rather fiscal convenience that led to the greater use of the Athenian coins throughout the arkhê. Thus, the increasing adoption of Attic currency was an organic development driven by the increasing integration of the Aegian economy.
>
> 2012: 22

Either way, it is impossible to overlook the ideological consequences of such a standardized coin in a world of multiple currencies.

58 On the importance of kinship in Greece, see Patterson:

> As we have seen, communities relied heavily on myth for the development of an identity within their walls, but its uses beyond also were myriad. Their relations with other Greek and with non-Greek communities were, in a sense, 'international'. *Sungenia*, the usual (but not universal) term the Greeks used to designate kinship, was a bond that opened doors, especially important as the Greek world was filled with enclaves of exclusivity known as *poleis*.
>
> 2010: 13

59 Bremmer (1997).

Chapter 3

1 For an account of this 'omnipresence' of the hero, see Stafford (2012), xxv–xxvi.
2 See Kennedy (2009) for examples of ideologically driven representations of Athena in Athens.
3 Boardman (1975b, 1982, 1989); see also Stafford (2012), 163–7.
4 Cf. Boardman (1975a).
5 See Hdt. 1.60.
6 There are multiple examples of this iconography, see, e.g., New York 17.230.14, Athens, NM 401 or Naples, Mus.Naz. 81177.
7 See Stafford (2012), 164–5, for the challenges to Boardman reading. See also Hannah (1995) for a challenge to this view.
8 For counter-arguments and criticism on the associations of Heracles and Pisistratus in Boardman, see Cook (1987).
9 Holt relates this transformation to a shift in rhetoric: 'Philosophers begin to transfer his greatness from the physical to the moral plane, following Prodikos' Sunday-school allegory about the choice which the young Herakles makes between Virtue and Vice (Xen., *Mem.* ii 1.21–34)' (1989: 79–8).

10 For examples of this iconography, see MuM Sonderliste R (1977) no. 22: Heidelberg P, Berlin (West), Staatl. Mus. V. I. 3151, Paris, Louvre CA 598 or Madrid, Arch. Mus. 10915.
11 See Boardman (1975a) with figures.
12 See, e.g., Amsterdam, Allard Pierson 3505, London BM E 227 or Paris, Petit Palais 327.
13 Cf. n. 6.
14 See LIMC, 'Herakles'.
15 See Stafford (2012), 164–5; Boardman (1975a).
16 For an extensive description of Heracles' cults, see Gruppe (1918) in RE, and in Attica, see Woodford (1966).
17 Cf. Boardman 'Heracles' in LIMC. For a general introduction to the cult of Heracles in Greece, see Larson (2021).
18 For a full list of evidence of Heracles and Athena, see Deacy (2005) and *LIMC*. For the special relation between Heracles and Athena, see Shapiro (1989), 159 ff.
19 Larson: '[Heracles] was certainly the earliest of the heroes to achieve Panhellenic fame, and this universal popularity pre-dates the formation of the Greek city-states and the dissemination of the Homeric epic' (2009: 31). Larson: 'Herakles is unique among Greek heroes. He achieved Panhellenic status at such an early date that his origins can no longer be traced. (. . .) Unlike most heroic figures, Herakles was the exclusive possession of no single city or village' (2007: 183).
20 Pindar, e.g., links Heracles to manly achievements, cf. *Isth*. iv. 11–12.
21 Cf. Parke (1977), 23, 82–3.
22 Cf., e.g., Marathon and Cynosarges below.
23 For a complete list of Heracles titles in cult, see Gruppe (1918), in RE, 1000–4.
24 Cf. Verbank-Piérard (1992); and Parke: 'According to the popular picture of Heracles he was a hero who indulged greatly in eating and drinking. Hence his cult generally included feasting as a prominent element in the ritual, and at Kynosarges, as elsewhere also, to guarantee the god company at his meal twelve members were chosen as Parasitoi' (1977: 51).
25 Another characteristic of Heracles' cult, as Susan Woodford (1966) points out, is the four-column heracleion. Although it is never referred to in surviving texts. Vase paintings and some architectural remains attest to the existence of such a building.
26 Aristotle, *Ath. Pol.* 54.7; IG 1^3.2.
27 Cf. Hdt. 6.108, 116.
28 See Paus. 1.15.2, 1.32.4.
29 Cf. Ferguson (1938).

30 Ibid., 5 and 7.
31 Stafford (2012), 175.
32 Larson (2009), 36.
33 Ekroth (2009), 138.
34 Larson:

> the first firmly attested cults of Herakles appeared during the seventh century when the Greek city-state had already emerged. Developing city-states announced their identities through the promotion of local festivals and the construction of monumental temples to their patron deities, but little of this energy was expended on Herakles, perhaps because he belonged to every city and none. (...) Yet his cult required no state sponsorship to ensure their propagation.
>
> 2009: 35–6

35

> αὐτὸς γὰρ Κρονίων καλλιστεφάνου πόσις Ἥρης
> Ζεὺς Ἡρακλείδαις ἄστυ δέδωκε τόδε. (fr.2.West)
>
> Since the son of Chronos, husband to the fair-crowned Hera,
> Zeus himself had given this city to Heracles.

36 Cf., e.g., Walker (1995); Mills (1997).
37 Hooker: 'At the heart of this "state" propaganda lay the Spartan teaching about the origin of the city: specifically the connection of the royal houses with the sons of Heracles' (1989: 122).
38 Cf. Boardman (1975b) on the importance of Peisistratus on the creation of this myth.
39 Nilsson:

> The mysteries, which probably come down from the mycenean age, were rooted in the soil and could not be transferred to another place. (...) A branch cult was founded in Athens, the Eleusion north of the Areopagus, where theoxenia were brought to Plouton and Persephone under the supervision of the hierophant (note *IG*, II², 1933). Of course, the Athenians adopted the usual means of instituting a procession from the ruling city to the cult place, but this procession is singular in so far as there was also a procession from Eleusis to Athens.
>
> 1986: 38

40 Mylonas (1962), 103–4.
41 Boardman (1975b), 6.
42 See Healey (1990), chapter 1, for the importance of the Eleusian Games.
43 Cf. ibid., 266.

44 On the revival of the festival as an act of counter-propaganda, see Hornblower (1992), 194 ff. On Delos and Euripides choral odes, see Henrichs (1996); on Delos and the possible connections with Cleon politics, see Brock (1996).
45 Shapiro (1989); Boardman (1975a).
46 Boardman (1975a), 7; and Shapiro (1989), 80. Shapiro believes this interpretation keeps within an Athenian attempt to broaden the scope of the sanctuary:

> if this interpretation of the *reggio* amphora is correct, the scene in the belly reflects several purely Athenian traditions, in an Athenian setting. This is fully in keeping with Athens' policy probably throughout the sixth century and onto the fifth, of co-opting a once local cult at Eleusis and turning it into a Panhellenic one administered from Athens.
>
> 1989: 80

47 See Parker (1996), 142–3, on the Panhellenism of the Holy Mysteries and also on the Panathenaica, whose Panhellenism has less evidence and would have been more relevant for the allies of the Delian League.
48 Cavanaugh (1996), 94; see also Clinton (2008), 5 ff. The importance of this myth made it to the rhetoric of the city and was added to one of the qualities of Athens as it is attested by Isocrates (*Paneg.* 28–9).
49 See Healey (1990), 264.
50 Translation: Sakurai and Raubitchek (1987), 264; see also Clinton (2008), 21 ff.
51 The hero is also the subject of one Homeric Hymn (15), but the hymn is probably Hellenistic.
52 *The Shield*: for a discussion of the date and eventual relationships with art, see Cook (1937) and Shapiro (1984) on the dependence of iconography on the *Shield*. Heracles was also the centre of some lost or fragmentary poems, namely the *Heracleia* of Pisander of Rhodes, the *Sack of Oichalia* of Creophylus of Samos and in three poems from Stesichorus: *Kyknos*, *Cerberus* and *Geryoneis*.
53 Cf. Rozokoki: 'the role of Athena in the Geryoneis must, I believe, have been particularly active' (2009: 3). For a discussion of the fragments, see Page (1973).
54 Papadopoulou: 'Heracles, the Greek hero par excellence, holds an outstanding position. Apart from the gods (among which Pindar has his own preferences), of all of his heroes, Heracles is, beyond all doubt, his favourite figure' (2005: 76).
55 See, e.g., Pindar, *Ol.* x. 20–30, *Nem.* i.61–3.
56 See Nieto Hernadez (1993).
57 On Heracles in Athenian Drama, see Woodford (1966), 49–115; Galinsky (1972), 40–100; and Silk (1985).
58 Cf. Winnington-Ingram (1980), 300.

59 See fr. 936 Cropp possibly from a Pirithous for a reference to the descent of Heracles into Hades. fr. 863 Cropp from an uncertain satyr play, for another possible reference to the same myth.
60 For an approach to Theseus and politics in Attic tragedy, see Mills (1997).
61 Osborne (2012), agreeing with Hall (2009), points out the political relevance of this play:

> Deliberation and decision are part of the stock-in-trade of tragedy, but Trachiniae is notable among Sophoclean tragedies for this explicit consultation with the chorus and for the way in which events – the arrival of Lichas, impinge upon and alter the decision-making (though comparable is Euripides' *Hippolytus*, as also for the precipitation of Hyllus cursing, ll. 807–12). Within Athenian politics the decision to execute all the men of Mytilene is marked as ill-considered by its subsequent reversal under the pressure of Diodotus, who warns that speed and passion are inimical to good decision-making (*Th.* 3.42.1). But second thoughts were a regular feature of Athenian politics – as we see with the second thoughts about the wisdom of going to war with Sparta at all (*Th.* 2.59.1–2).
>
> Osborne (2012: 280–1)

62 Cf. Fowler (1999).
63 Hall (1997).
64 Woodford (1966).

Chapter 4

1 For an overview with bibliography on Delphi and the Athenian Agora, see Scott (2010) and Camp II and Mauzy (2009), respectively.
2 See Scott (2010).
3 For the importance of Delphi during the archaic and classical periods see, Morgan (1990) and Scott (2010) with bibliography.
4 See Defradas (1972), 123.
5 Quoted in Neer (2001), 284.
6 Olympia inv. B 2600.
7 See Neer (2004b).
8 See Chapter 3.
9 For a full description of the remaining fragments, see La Coste Messelière FdD IV.3; for a discussion of the themes with bibliography, see Fuchs and Floren (1987) and Neer (2004b).

10 See Stafford (2012), 42–5.
11 FdD III 4 190.
12 Scott (2010), 77.
13 For a full discussion of the sculptures of the Athenian treasury, see FdD IV.4.
14 For a discussion with recent bibliography, see Neer (2004b).
15 Ibid.
16 For the reframing of the memories of the Persian Wars made by individual cities, especially at Panhellenic spaces like Delphi, see Yates (2019).
17 See Scott (2010), 78–80.
18 Cf. Neer (2004b), 71–2.
19 Cf. ibid., 75.
20 Ibid., 79–80.
21 Ibid., 86, see (Paus. 10.10.1).
22 For an in-depth discussion of the iconography and construction, see Von der Hoff (2009) and Gensheimer (2017).
23 Von den Hoff (2009), 100.
24 For the importance of the Agora in Peisistratid times, see Anderson (2003).
25 Camp II and Mauzy (2009), 19–21.
26 For a discussion of the first placement of the statues of the Eponymous heroes, see Taylor (1991).
27 For a full discussion of the familial politics of Miltiades, Cimon and Pericles, see Connor (1992), 61.
28 For a description of Cimon's Athens, see Camp (2001), 63 ff.
29 For further details, see Chapter 3.
30 For the full description, see Paus. 1. 17, 2–3.
31 For a discussion with bibliography, see Castriota (1992), 33 n. 3.
32 Cf. ibid., 58.
33 See Stansbury-O'Donnell (2005), 74–5.
34 For a full account of the building's physical characteristics, see Meritt (1970).
35 That some shields were hung on the walls of the stoa is not questioned, although it has been stated that some of the shields normally thought to be in there could have been in the Nike Temple at the entrance to the Acropolis. See Schultz (2003).
36 For a full list of all the ancient sources on these paintings, see Harrison (1972).
37 For a full discussion on bibliography, see Stansbury-O'Donnell (2005) and Cruciani and Fiorini (1998), 32 ff.
38 One proponent of such an interpretation is Taylor (1998).
39 See Francis (1990), 91 ff.
40 Cf. Stansbury-O'Donnell (2005).

41 Kennedy: 'It was a process that could only have existed in Athens where pride in their victories over barbarian invaders was coupled with an even stronger investment in their democratic institutions' (2009: 65–6).
42 Cf. Castriota (2005), 91.
43 Ibid. (1992), 79; on the way the memories of the Persian Wars were filtered by the different poleis, see Yates (2019).
44 See Cruciani and Fiorini (1998), 41.
45 Cf. Thompson (1962).
46 Garland:

> without denying Kimon any loftier motives, the promotion of the cult of Theseus was thus a way of polishing up the family's tarnished image, a necessary precondition to Kimon's own political rise (...). In sum, the recovery of Theseus' bones was a carefully orchestrated drama which owed something to private and national interest, whatever it owed to instinctive piety.
>
> 1992: 85

On the importance of bone transferal and of Theseus to the domination of the Aegian territory, see Patterson (2010).

Chapter 5

1 Cf. Stafford (2012), 171.
2 See ibid., 3–4.
3 For the tradition of Heracles' connection with the Argonauts, see ibid., 55.
4 See Connor (1989), 20–1, on the use of *kallinikos* as echoes of the festival settings.
5 Griffin (1980), see Hom., *Il*. 15.607.
6 Cf. Papadopoulou (2005), 37 ff.
7 See Edwards (1991), 245–7.
8 See Hartigan (1987).
9 Silk:

> Her words, furthermore, suggest an identification with him (...). He is the killer and she is the killer, because she is both independent of him and an aspect of him. The staging makes her external; the words tend to suggest her internality; she is, therefore, both, even more clearly than other destructive deities of the psyche, like Dionysus in *Bacchae*. But it is not – to restate the point – that Heracles was 'mad all the time'. There is no psychological continuity between Heracles now and before.
>
> 1985: 16–17

10 While Bond (1981), 315, acknowledges the use of the verb elsewhere in tragedy, the Homeric connection is missing.
11 Cf. Papadopoulou (2005), 150.
12 Cf. Gregory (1991), 123–4.
13 For Heracles as an epinician hero, see Foley (1985), 177 ff.
14 Cf. Gregory (1977), 275.
15 See 170 ff., for Amphitryon defence of Heracles' arms as self-sufficient. On the arms of Heracles and contemporary reality, see Cohen (1994) and Vilariño Rodriguez (2010).
16 Cf. Galinsky (1972) and Woodford (1966).
17 Silk (1985), 4.
18 Friendship is an important theme in Euripides. For a discussion of the theme in *Orestes*, see Lourenço (1995).
19 For similarities between the two plays, see Michelini (1987), 234–5.
20 Sophocles, *Ajax* 330: ἀρήξατ' εἰσελθόντες, εἰ δύνασθέ τι. φίλων γὰρ οἱ τοιοίδε νικῶνται λόγοις. Τέκμησσα, δεινοῖς, παῖ Τελεύταντος, λέγεις. Sophocles, *Ajax* 349: φίλοι ναυβάται, μόνοι ἐμῶν φίλων μόνοι ἔτ' ἐμμένοντες ὀρθῷ νόμῳ.
21 Cf. Papadopoulou (2005), 80.
22 See Finglass (2011), 49, despite not finding much to support the view of Ajax as a cult hero in this play, Finglass supports this moment as a manifestation of the cultic aspect of the hero.

Chapter 6

1 Cf. Said (1993). Last, but not least, Delphi where Apollo drives out the pollution of matricide with the purification of a slain swine disappears as a necessary stage on the way to Athens: Orestes goes straight 'across the Isthmian narrow towards the happy hill in Cecrops' land' (1288–9).
2 Meiggs: '[the control of the Spartans over Delphi] may be one of the reasons that prompted the renewal of Athens' concern for Delos in the winter of 426–425, when they carried through a further purification and revived the Delian festival' (1972: 300).
3 See Chapter 3.
4 For a full discussion of the gods in this play, with bibliography, see Yunis (1988), 139 ff.
5 On the role of Zeus in the play, see Mikalson (1986).
6 Cf. Gregory (1991), 139–40.

7 Griffiths (2006), 98.
8 On the discussion of the nature and understanding of the gods in Athens, see Yunis (1988).
9 Since at least Xenophanes, the portrait of Greek gods as presented in literature has been debated and criticized by various sophists and philosophers.
10 On the different ways the suppliant theme was subverted in this play, see Chapter 7.
11 Burnett: 'The escape of the suppliant family of Heracles evokes an outburst of conventional piety from the chorus, but it cannot have left the Athenian audience, drilled as it was in the nuances of tragic hubris and religious crime, feeling very comfortable' (1971: 166).
12 For example, Parker states: 'What Aeschylus presents instead is, in Eumenides, a vision of a just society in which men's vagrant desires are restrained by fear of punishment. Thus, ideally the citizens will never need to "learn through suffering": the city has thought in advance and embodies in its institutions the necessary restraints that will keep their minds healthy' (2009: 144).
13 Or despite the Areopagus. For a discussion on the role of the tribunal in the play, see Dover (1957), Samons (1999) and Kennedy (2006).
14 On the jurisdiction of the empire, see Meiggs (1972), 220–33. Meiggs: 'the work of proxenoi of Athens and of Athenian officials overseas was powerfully supplemented by the people's law-courts in Athens. the increasing use of Athenian courts to try allies' cases was one of the allies' main grievances; the dependence on courts rather than arbitrary purges was one of the Athenians' main defences of their rule' (ibid.: 219).[14]
15 Cf. verses 348 ff., 673 ff., 689 ff., 761–3 ff., 889 ff. and 1025 ff.
16 For more on the importance of chorus self-referentiality, see Henrichs (1994).
17 See 110–11, 348–59, 689–99.
18 Against, say, 12 in *Suppliant Women*, and these three references certainly pale into insignificance in comparison with the 14 in Sophocles' *Electra*.
19 For the use of Epinician in Euripides, see Kampakoglou, A. (2018).
20 E.g. Bond (1981), 146–50.
21 For a detailed analysis of the second stasimon as a eulogy, see Parry (1965).
22 Zeitlin: 'Events in Thebes and the characters who enact them both fascinate and repel the audience, finally instructing the spectator as to how their city might refrain from imitating the Theban negative example' (1990: 145).
23 As Hall notes,

> Other Athenians in tragedy usually display virtue, piety, and respect for suppliants and the democratic principle of freedom of speech: this is a particularly revealing aspect of what might be called the Athenians' self-regarding use of tragedy as 'moral

aetiology'. On the rare occasions when Athenians do misbehave or act foolishly in tragedy it is conspicuous that they are removed from their city for the duration of their misadventure. (...) Even Theseus in *Hippolytus*, who although no bad man is precipitate in judgement and unfair to his son, is a resident of Trozen in the Peloponnese for the duration and purposes of the play.

1997: 103

24 See, e.g., Isocrates 4.63.
25 Zeitlin: 'On the other hand, only in Athens, where the outsiders may enter into a new status through rituals of supplication and political rights of residency, can Oedipus himself transcend human time; crossing the boundary between the living and the dead, he can make permanent his value to the city in the institution of the hero cult' (1990: 166).
26 Rehm (2002: 102) has suggested one more way in which the space is fundamental in this play: the importance of bodies of water – chaos dominates the world of the labours. Bodies of water, as untamed as they are in the ancient world, often represent chaos. I think this helps to deepen the image of Thebes as the space of chaos and where redemption is impossible, as opposed to Athens. Burnett also noted that these bodies of water are now polluted (1971: 167–8 on vv. 780 ff).
27 See Rehm (2002), 103 ff.
28 Sinn:

But the sanctuaries themselves were protected by asylia. One of the basic tenets of Greek religion was that everything inside sacred territory was owned by the god – and the possessions of divinities were of course taboo for human beings. Hence every sanctuary had the status of an inviolable percent (asylon hieron). The inviolability of the sanctuaries guaranteed pilgrims and festival participants security. In the same way it served to protect the often valuable votive offerings. The sanctuaries were predestined to fulfil other functions by virtue of the security afforded by asylia. For example they could perform the function of banks. The sanctuary of Artemis in Ephesus is the most noteworthy example of this. Thanks to its status of inviolability the Sacred Island of Delos became one of the most important trading centres of the Mediterranean.

1993: 90–1

29 Cf. Burnett (1971), 165.
30 Papadopoulou (2005), 194, despite the Athenocentric emphasis or the patriotic tone of the drama, it is Heracles who remains the focus of the drama throughout. The insight into human life that his suffering has given him is an experience that Theseus cannot fully grasp, no matter how enlightened he is.

31 Cf. Rehm (2002), 35.
32 Foley: 'In the *Heracles* Euripides systematically confronts almost the entire earlier tradition on Heracles and the contradictions it poses for a Thebes that finds no place for the hero. Yet, finally, only Athens and tragedy, with its emphasis on sacrifice, violence and suffering can rescue Heracles from the "death"' (1985: 150).

Conclusion

1 Cf. Plutarch, *Nicias* 3.
2 Cf. Plutarch, *Alcibiades* 11.
3 There is no certain date for the play. I follow Bond (1981), xxx–xxxii, in placing the play some time around 416–414 BC.
4 Cf. Low:

> The sanctuary is the god's share of the territory of the polis, and by the grant of a parcel of land the divinity becomes, as it were, part of the polis. By these means one might say, the sacred is configured in political terms. As the ruler, the god has both rights and responsibilities (...). The relationship to the sacred, thus, is framed in terms of fair exchange.
>
> 2005: 222

5 Cf. Turner (2006), 236.
6 See Meiggs (1972), 220–33.

Bibliography

Abbreviations

APGRD   Archive of Performances of Greek and Roman Drama, University of Oxford
FCT   Fundação para a Ciência e Tecnologia, Portugal
FdD   *Fouilles de Delphes*, École française d'Athènes
IG   *Inscriptiones Graecae*
LIMC   *Lexicon Iconographicum Mythologiae Classicae*
OCD3   *Oxford Classical Dictionary* (3rd edn)
RE   *The Realencyclopädie der Classischen Altertumswissenschaft*

Published and unpublished sources

Allan, W., and A. Kelly (2013). 'Listening to Many Voices: Athenian Tragedy as Popular Art'. In *The Author's Voice in Classical and Late Antiquity*, ed. A. Marmodoro and J. Hill, 77–122. Oxford: Oxford University Press.

Anderson, G. (2003). *The Athenian Experiment: Building an Imagined Political Community in Ancient Attica, 508–490 BC*. Ann Arbor, MI: University of Michigan Press.

Arendt, H. (2004). *The Origins of Totalitarianism*. 1st edn. New York.

Athanassaki, L. (2010). 'Performing Myth through Word, Deed, and Image: The Gigantomachy in Euripides' Ion'. In *Mito y Performance. De Grecia a la Modernidad. Quinto Coloquio Internacional. Acta*, ed. A. M. Gonzalez de Tobia, 199–242. La Plata: Facultad de Humanidades y Ciencias de la Educación (UNLP).

Athanassaki, L. (2011). 'Song, Politics, and Cultural Memory: Pindar's Pythian 7 and the Alcmaeonid Temple of Apollo'. *Archaic and Classical Choral Song: Performance, Politics and Dissemination*, 10: 235.

Athanassaki, L. (2018). 'Talking Thalassocracy in 5th-Century Athens: From Bacchylides 17th and Cimonian Monuments to Euripides' Troades'. In *Paths of Song: The Lyric Dimension of Greek Tragedy*, ed. R. Andujar, T. Coward and Th. Hadjimichael, 87–117. Berlin: de Gruyter.

Barbato, M. (2020). *Ideology of Democratic Athens: Institutions, Orators and the Mythical Past*. Edinburgh: Edinburgh University Press.

Barlow, S. (1982). 'Structure and Dramatic Realism in Euripides' "Heracles"'. *Greece & Rome*, 29 (2): 115–25.

Barlow, S. (1993). 'Structure and Dramatic Realism in Euripides' *Heracles*'. In *Greek Tragedy*, ed. I. McAuslan and P. Walcot, 193–203. Oxfrd: Oxford University Press.

Barlow, S. (1998). *Euripides Heracles*. Warminster: Aris & Phillips.

Barron, J. P. (1962). 'Milesian Politics and Athenian Propaganda'. *Journal of Hellenic Studies*, 82: 1–6.

Barron, J. P. (1964). 'Religious Propaganda of the Delian League'. *Journal of Hellenic Studies*, 84: 35–48.

Barthes, R. (1974). *S/Z*. New York: Hill and Wang.

Boardman, J. (1974). *Athenian Black Figure Vases*. New York: Thames and Hudson (World of Art Library).

Boardman, J. (1975a). *Athenian Red Figure Vases: The Archaic Period: A Handbook*. London: Thames and Hudson.

Boardman, J. (1975b). 'Herakles, Peisistratos and Eleusis'. *Journal of Hellenic Studies*, 95: 1–12.

Boardman, J. (1982). 'Herakles, Theseus and Amazons'. *The Eye of Greece: Studies in the Art of Athens*, ed. D. Kurtz and B. Sparkes, 1–28. Cambridge: Cambridge University Press.

Boardman, J. (1985). *Greek Sculpture: Classical Period*. London; Thames and Hudson.

Boardman, J. (1989). 'Herakles, Peisistratos, and the Unconvinced'. *Journal of Hellenic Studies*, 109: 158–9.

Boardman, J. (2001). *The History of Greek Vases: Potters, Painters and Pictures*. London: Thames and Hudson.

Boedeker, D. (2009). 'Athenian Religion in the Age of Pericles'. In *The Cambridge Companion to the Age of Pericles*, ed. L. J. Samons II, 46–69. Cambridge: Cambridge University Press.

Boedeker, D., and K. A. Raaflaub, eds (1998). *Democracy, Empire, and the Arts in Fifth-Century Athens*. Cambridge, MA: Harvard University Press.

Bond, G., ed. (1981). *Euripides: Heracles*. Oxford: Oxford University Press.

Bremmer, J. N. (1987). *Interpretations of Greek Mythology*. London: Routledge.

Bremmer, J. N. (1997). 'Myth as Propaganda: Athens and Sparta'. *Zeitschrift Fur Papyrologie Und Epigraphik*, 117: 9–17.

Brock, R. (1996). 'Thucydides and the Athenian Purification of Delos'. *Mnemosyne*, 49 (3): 321–7.

Burnett, A. (1971). *Catastrophe Survived : Euripides' Plays of Mixed Reversal*. Oxford: Oxford University Press.

Calame, C. (2003). *Myth and History in Ancient Greece the Symbolic Creation of a Colony*. Princeton, NJ: Princeton University Press.

Camp, J. M. (2001). *The Archaeology of Athens*. New Haven, CT: Yale University Press.

Camp II, J. M., and C. A. Mauzy (2009). *The Athenian Agora: New Perspectives on an Ancient Site*. Athens: American School of Classical Studies at Athens; and Mainz am Rhein: Verlag Philipp von Zabern.

Carter, D. M., ed. (2011). *Why Athens? A Reappraisal of Tragic Politics*. Oxford: Oxford University Press.

Castriota, D. (1992). *Myth, Ethos, and Actuality*. Madison, WI: University of Wisconsin Press.

Castriota, D. (2005). 'Feminizing the Barbarian and Barbarizing the Feminine: Amazons, Trojans, and Persians in the Stoa Poikile'. In *Periklean Athens and Its Legacy: Problems and Perspectives*, ed. J. M. Barringer and J. M. Hurwit and J. J. Pollitt, 89–102. Austin, TX: University of Texas Press.

Cavalier, K. (1995). 'Did Not Potters Portray Peisistratos Posthumously as Herakles?'. *Electronic Antiquity*, 2 (5). Available online: https://scholar.lib.vt.edu/ejournals/ElAnt/V2N5/cavalier.html (accessed 31 July 2015).

Cavanaugh, M. (1996). *Eleusis and Athens: Documents in Finance, Religion, and Politics in the Fifth Century B.C.* Atlanta, GA: Scholars Press.

Clarke, D. (1977). *Spatial Archaeology*. London: Academic Press.

Clinton, K. (2008). *Eleusis, the Inscriptions on Stone: Documents of the Sanctuary of the Two Goddesses and Public Documents of the Deme*. Athens: Archaeological Society at Athens.

Cohen, B. (1994). 'From Bowman to Clubman: Herakles and Olympia'. *The Art Bulletin*, 76 (4): 695–715.

Conacher, D. J. (1955). 'Theme, Plot, and Technique in the "Heracles" of Euripides'. *Phoenix*, 9 (4): 139–52.

Conacher, D. J. (1967). *Euripidean Drama: Myth, Theme and Structure*. Toronto: University of Toronto Press.

Connor, W. R. (1989). 'City Dionysia and Athenian Democracy'. *Classica et mediaevalia*, 40: 7–32.

Connor, W. R. (1992). *The New Politicians of Fifth-Century Athens*. Indianapolis, IN: Hackett Publishing.

Cook, R. M. (1937). 'The Date of the Hesiodic Shield'. *Classical Quarterly*, 31: 204–14.

Cook, R. M. (1987). 'Pots and Pisistratan Propaganda'. *Journal of Hellenic Studies*, 107: 167–9.

Cruciani, C., and L. Fiorini (1998). *I Modelli Del Moderato La Stoà Poikile e l'Hephaisteion Di Atene Nel Programma Edilizio Cimoniano*. Napoli: Edizioni scientifiche italiane.

Deacy, S. J. (2005). 'Herakles and His "Girl": Heroism, Athena and Beyond'. In *Herakles and Hercules: Exploring a Graeco-Roman Divinity*, ed. L. Rawlings and H. Bowden, 37–50. Swansea: Classical Press of Wales.

Defradas, J. (1972). *Les Thèmes de la propagande Delphique*. 2e tirage. Paris: Librairie C. Klincksieck.

Diggle, J. (OCT) (1981). *Euripidis fabulae* (Scriptorum classicorum bibliotheca Oxoniensis). Oxonii: E typographeo Clarendoniano.

Dinsmoor, W. (1921). 'Attic Building Accounts. IV: The Statue of Athena Promachos'. *American Journal of Archaeology*, 25 (2): 118–29.

Dover, K. J. (1957). 'The Political Aspect of Aeschylus's Eumenides'. *Journal of Hellenic Studies*, 77 (2): 230–7.

Dunn, F. M. (1996). *Tragedy's End: Closure and Innovation in Euripidean Drama*. New York and Oxford: Oxford University Press.

Dušanić, S. (1980–1). 'Athens, Crete and the Aegean After 366/5 B.C.'. *Talanta*, 12–13: 7–30.

Eastman, H. (2010). 'Hercules'. Manuscript of the play first produced 20 July.

Edwards, M. W. (1991). *The Iliad: A Commentary. Volume V: Books 17–20*. Cambridge: Cambridge University Press.

Ekroth, G. (2009). 'The Cult of Heroes'. In *Heroes: Mortals and Myths in Ancient Greece*, 120–43. Baltimore, MD: Walters Art Museum.

Ellul, J. (1973). *Propaganda: The Formation of Men's Attitudes*, trans. K. Kellen and J. Lerner, with an introduction by K. Kellen. New York: Vintage Books.

Evans, J. (1992). *The Art of Persuasion: Political Propaganda from Aeneas to Brutus*. Ann Arbor, MI. University of Michigan Press.

Evans, N. (2010). *Civic Rites: Democracy and Religion in Ancient Athens*. Berkeley and Los Angeles, CA: University of California Press.

Evans, R. (2017). *Mass and Elite in the Greek and Roman Worlds*. London and New York: Routledge.

Ferguson, W. (1938). 'The Salaminoi of Heptaphylai and Sounion'. *Hesperia*, 7: 1–76.

Finglass, P. J., ed. (2011). *Sophocles: Ajax*, vol. 48. Cambridge: Cambridge University Press.

Fischer-Lichte, E. (2009). 'Culture as Performance'. *Modern Austrian Literature*, 42 (3): 1–10.

Fischer-Lichte, E. (2010). 'Performance as Event–Reception as Transformation'. *Theorising Performance: Greek Drama, Cultural History and Critical Practice*, 29–42. London and New York: Bloomsbury.

Fisher, N., and Van Wees, H., eds (2015). *Aristocracy in Antiquity: Redefining Greek and Roman Elites*. Llandysul: Classical Press of Wales.

Foley, H. P. (1985). *Ritual Irony: Poetry and Sacrifice in Euripides*. Ithaca, NY: Cornell University Press.

Fowler, R. L. H. (1999). 'Three Places of the Trachiniae'. In *Sophocles Revisited: Essays Presented to Sir Hugh Lloyd-Jones*, ed. J. Griffin, 161–75. Oxford: Oxford University Press.

Francis, E. D. (1990). *Image and Idea in Fifth Century Greece: Art and Literature After the Persian Wars*. London: Routledge.

Fuchs, W., and J. Floren (1987). *Die Griechische Plastik. Bd.1 Die Geometrische Und Archäische Plastik*. München: Beck.

Galinsky, K. (1972). *The Herakles Theme: The Adaptations of the Hero in Literature from Homer to the Twentieth Century*. Oxford: Blackwell.

Garland, R. (1992). *Introducing New Gods: The Politics of Athenian Religion*. Ithaca, NY: Cornell University Press.

Gensheimer, M. B. (2017). 'Metaphors for Marathon in the Sculptural Program of the Athenian Treasury at Delphi'. *Hesperia*, 86 (1): 1–42.

Goldhill, S. (1987). 'The Great Dionysia and Civic Ideology'. *Journal of Hellenic Studies*, 107: 58.

Goldhill, S. (1999). 'Programme Notes'. In *Performance Culture and Athenian Democracy*, ed. S. Goldhill, S., and R. Osborne, 1–30. Cambridge: Cambridge University Press.

Goldhill, S. (2000a). 'Civic Ideology and the Problem of Difference: The Politics of Aeschylean Tragedy, Once Again. *Journal of Hellenic Studies*, 120: 34–56.

Goldhill, S. (2000b). Greek Drama and Political Theory. In *The Cambridge History of Greek and Roman Political Thought*, ed. C. J. Rowe, M. Schofield, S. Harrison and M. S. Lane, 60–88. Cambridge: Cambridge University Press.

Goldhill, S., and R. Osborne, eds (1999). *Performance Culture and Athenian Democracy*. Cambridge: Cambridge University Press.

Gregory, J. (1977). 'Euripides' Heracles'. *Yale Classical Studies*, 25: 259–7.

Gregory, J. (1991). *Euripides and the Instruction of the Athenians*. Ann Arbor, MI: University of Michigan Press.

Grene, D., and R. A. Lattimore (1959). *The Complete Greek Tragedies*. Chicago, IL: University oof Chicago Press.

Griffin, J. (1980). *Homer on Life and Death*. Oxford: Clarendon Press.

Griffin, J. (1998). 'The Social function of Attic Tragedy'. *Classical Quarterly*, New Series, 48 (1): 39–61.

Griffith, M. and D. M. Carter (2011). 'Introduction'. In *Why Athens? A Reappraisal of Tragic Politics*, ed. D. M. Carter, 1–16. Oxford: Oxford University Press.

Griffiths, E. (2006). *Euripides: Heracles*. London: Duckworth.

Hall, E. (1997). 'The Sociology of Athenian Tragedy'. In *The Cambridge Companion to Greek Tragedy*, ed. P. E. Easterling, 93–126. Cambridge: Cambridge University Press.

Hall, E. (2009). 'Deianeira Deliberates: Precipitate Decision-Making and Trachiniae'. In *Sophocles and the Greek Tragic Tradition*, ed. S. Goldhill and E. Hall, 69–96. Cambridge: Cambridge University Press.

Halliwell, F. S., A. Sommerstein, J. Henderson and B. Zimmermann (1993). *Tragedy, Comedy and the Polis*, Papers from the Greek Drama Conference, Nottingham, 18–20 July 1990. Bari: Levante Editori.

Hamilton, R. (1985). 'Slings and Arrows: The Debate with Lycus in the Heracles'. *Transactions of the American Philological Association*, 115: 19–25.

Hannah, R. (1995). 'Peisistratos, the Peisistratids and the Introduction of Herakles to Olympos: An Alternative Scenario'. *Electronic Antiquity*, 2 (5). Available online: https://scholar.lib.vt.edu/ejournals/ElAnt/V3N2/hannah.html (accessed 31 July 2015).

Hansen, M. H., and T. H. Nielsen (2004). *An Inventory of Archaic and Classical Poleis: An Investigation*. Oxford: Oxford University Press.

Harrison, E. (1972). 'The South Frieze of the Nike Temple and the Marathon Painting in the Painted Stoa'. *American Journal of Archaeology*, 76 (4): 353–78.

Harter, D. L., and J. Sullivan (1953). *Propaganda Handbook*. Media, PA: 20th Century Publishing.

Hartigan, K. (1987). 'Euripidean Madness: Herakles and Orestes'. *Greece & Rome*, 34 (2): 126–35.

Haubold, J. (2000). *Homer's People: Epic Poetry and Social Formation*. Caambridge: Cambridge University Press.

Healey, R. F. (1990). *Eleusinian Sacrifices in the Athenian Law Code*. New York: Garland Publishing.

Henderson, J. (2007). 'Drama and Democracy'. In *The Cambridge Companion to the Age of Pericles*, ed. L. J. Samons II, 179–95. Cambridge: Cambridge University Press.

Henrichs, A. (1994). '"Why Should I Dance?": Choral Self-Referentiality in Greek Tragedy'. *Arion: A Journal of Humanities and the Classics*, Third Series, 3 (1): 56–111.

Henrichs, A (1996). 'Dancing in Athens, Dancing on Delos: Some Patterns of Choral Projection in Euripides'. *Philologus*, 140 (1): 48–62.

Hölscher, T. (1998). 'Images and Political Identity: The Case of Athens'. In *Democracy, Empire, and the Arts in Fifth-Century Athens,* ed. D. Boedeker and K. A. Raaflaub, 15–42. Cambridge, MA: Harvard University Press.

Holt, P. (1989). 'The End of the Trachiniai and the Fate of Herakles'. *Journal of Hellenic Studies*, 109: 69–80.

Hooker, J. T. (1989). 'Spartan Propaganda'. In *Classical Sparta: Techniques Behind Her Success*. London: Routledge.

Hornblower, S. (1992). 'The Religious Dimension to the Peloponnesian War, or, What Thucydides does not Tell Us'. *Harvard Studies in Classical Philology*, 94: 169–97.

Hornblower, S., and A. Spawforth (2003). *The Oxford Classical Dictionary*. Rev. 3rd edn. Oxford: Oxford University Press.

Jackall, R. (1995). *Propaganda*. New York: New York University Press.

Jauss, H. R. (1982). *Aesthetic Experience and Literary Hermeneutics*. Minneapolis, MN: University of Minnesota Press.

Jauss, H., and T. Bahti (1982). *Toward an Aesthetic of Reception*. Theory and History of Literature, Vol. 2. Minneapolis, MN: University of Minnesota Press.

Jebb, R. C., P. Easterling, gen. ed., and introd. by B. Goward (2004). *Sophocles: Plays. Trachiniae*. New edn. London: Bristol Classical Press.

Jouanna, J., and Montanari, F., ed. (2009). *Eschyle à l'aube du théâtre occidental: Neuf exposés suivis de discussions: Vandoeuvres–Genève, 25–29 août 2008. Entretiens sur l'Antiquité classique*. Genève: Hardt.

Jowett, G. S., and V. J. O'Donnell (2006). *Propaganda and Persuasion*. 4th edn. Thousand Oaks, CA: Sage.

Kallet, L. (1998). 'Accounting for Culture in Fifth-Century Athens'. In *Democracy, Empire, and the Arts in Fifth-Century Athens*, ed. D. Boedeker and K. A. Raaflaub, 43–58. Cambridge, MA: Harvard University Press.

Kamerbeek, J. C. (1966). 'Unity and Meaning of Euripides "Heracles"'. *Mnemosyne*, 19 (1): 1–16.

Kampakoglou, A. (2018). 'Epinician Discourse in Euripides' Tragedies: The Case of Alexandros'. In *Paths of Song: The Lyric Dimension of Greek Tragedy*, ed. R. Andújar, T. Coward and T. Hadjimichael, 187–218. Berlin and Boston, MA: De Gruyter.

Kennedy, R. F. (2006). 'Justice, Geography and Empire in Aeschylus' Eumenides'. *Classical Antiquity*, 25 (1): 35–72.

Kennedy, R. F. (2009). *Athena's Justice: Athena, Athens and the Concept of Justice in Greek Tragedy*. New York: Peter Lang.

Kroll, J. (2009). 'What about Coinage?'. In *Interpreting the Athenian Empire*, ed. J. Ma, N. Papazarkadas and R. Parker, 195–209. London: Bloomsbury Publishing.

Larson, J. (2007). 'A Land Full of Gods: Nature Deities in Greek Religion'. In *A Companion to Greek Religion*, ed. D. Ogden, 56–70. Malden, MA, and Oxford: Blackwell.

Larson, J. (2009). 'The Singularity of Herakles'. In *Heroes: Mortals and Myths in Ancient Greece*, 31–8. Baltimore, MD: Walters Art Museum.

Larson, J. (2021). 'The Greek Cult of Heracles'. *The Oxford Handbook of Heracles*, ed. D. Ogden, 447–63. Oxford: Oxford University Press.

Levett, B. (2004). *Sophocles: Women of Trachis*. London: Bristol Classical Press.

Loraux, N. (1990a). 'Herakles: The Super-Male and the Feminine'. In *Before Sexuality: The Construction of Erotic Experience in the Ancient Greek World*, ed. D. M. Halperin, J. J. Winkler and F. I. Zeitlin, 21–52. Princeton, NJ: Princeton University Press.

Loraux, N. (1990b). 'Kreousa the Autochthon: A Study of Euripides' Ion'. In *Nothing to Do with Dionysos?*, ed. J. J. Winkler and F. I. Zeitlin, 168–206. Princeton, NJ: Princeton University Press.

Loraux, N. (1994). *The Children of Athena: Athenian Ideas about Citizenship and the Division between the Sexes*. Trans. C. Levine. Princeton, NJ: Princeton University Press.

Loraux, N. (2000). *Born of the Earth: Myth and Politics in Athens*. Ithaca, NY: Cornell University Press.

Loraux, N. (2006). *The Invention of Athens: The Funeral Oration in the Classical City*. Trans. A. Sheridan. New York: Zone Books.

Lourenço, F. (1995). 'À Excepção De Pílades?' Bons e Maus Φίλοι No Orestes De Euripides'. In *Colóquio Eros e Philia Na Cultura Grega*, ed. A. A. Nascimento, V. J. V. Jabouille and F. Lourenço, 145–50. Lisboa: Euphrosyne – Centro de Estudos Clássicos.

Low, P. (2005). 'Looking for the Language of Athenian Imperialism'. *Journal of Hellenic Studies*, 125: 93–111.

Lyne, R. O. A. M. (1987). *Further Voices in Vergil's Aeneid*. Oxford: Clarendon Press.

McCauley, B. (1999). 'Heroes and Power: The Politics of Bone Transferal'. In *Ancient Greek Hero Cult: Proceedings of the Fifth International Seminar on Ancient Greek Cult*, ed. Robin Hägg, 85–98. Stockholm: Svenska Institutet i Athen.

Meiggs, R. (1972). *The Athenian Empire*. Oxford: Oxford University Press.

Meritt, L. (1970). 'The Stoa Poikile'. *Hesperia*, 39 (4): 233–64.

Michelini, A. (1987). *Euripides and the Tragic Tradition*. Madison, WI. University of Wisconsin Press.

Mikalson, J. D. (1986). 'Zeus the Father and Heracles the Son in Tragedy'. *Transactions of the American Philological Association*, 116: 89–98.

Mills, S. (1997). *Theseus, Tragedy, and the Athenian Empire*. Oxford: Oxford University Press.

Morgan, C. (1990). *Athletes and Oracles: The Transformation of Olympia and Delphi in the Eighth Century BC*. Cambridge: Cambridge University Press.

Mylonas, G. (1962). *Eleusis and the Eleusinian Mysteries*. London: Routledge and Kegan Paul.

Nagy, G. (1996). *Poetry as Performance: Homer and Beyond*. Cambridge and New York: Cambridge University Press.

Neer, R. (2001). 'Framing the Gift: The Politics of the Siphnian Treasury at Delphi'. *Classical Antiquity*, 20 (2): 273–344.

Neer, R. (2004a). 'Reaction and Response'. *Critical Inquiry*, 30 (2): 472–6.

Neer, R. (2004b). 'The Athenian Treasury at Delphi and the Material of Politics'. *Classical Antiquity*, 23 (1): 63–94.

Neer, R., and L. Kurke (2019). *Pindar, Song, and Space: Towards a Lyric Archaeology*. Baltimore, MD: Johns Hopkins University Press.

Neils, J. (2007). 'Myth and Greek Art: Creating a Visual Language'. In *The Cambridge Companion to Greek Mythology*, ed. R. D. Woodard, 286–304. Cambridge: Cambridge University Press.

Nieto Hernadez, M. P. (1993). 'Heracles and Pindar'. *Mètis*, 8: 75–102.

Nilsson, M. P. (1986). *Cults, Myths, Oracles, and Politics in Ancient Greece: With Two Appendices: The Ionian Phylae, the Phratries*. Göte: P. Åström.

Nussbaum, M. (1986). *Fragility of Goodness: Luck and Ethics in Greek Tragedy and Philosophy*. Cambridge: Cambridge University Press.

Ober, J. (1989). *Mass and Elite in Democratic Athens: Rhetoric, Ideology, and the Power of the People*. Princeton, NJ: Princeton University Press.

Ober, J. (1996). *The Athenian Revolution: Essays on Ancient Greek Democracy and Political Theory*. Princeton, NJ: Princeton University Press.

Ober, J. (2008). *Democracy and Knowledge: Innovation and Learning in Classical Athens*. Princeton, NJ: Princeton University Press.

Ogden, D. (2021). *The Oxford Handbook of Heracles*. Oxford: Oxford University Press.

Osborne, R. (1999). 'Archaeology and the Athenian Empire'. *Transactions of the American Philological Association*, 129: 319–32.

Osborne, R. (2010). *Athens and Athenian Democracy*. Cambridge: Cambridge University Press.

Osborne, R. (2012). 'Sophocles and Contemporary Politics'. In *A Companion to Sophocles*, ed. K. Ormand, 270–86. Oxford: Wiley Blackwell.

Page, D. (1973). 'Stesichorus: The Geryoneïs'. *Journal of Hellenic Studies*, 93: 138–59.

Papadimitropoulos, L. (2008). 'Heracles as Tragic Hero'. *Classical World*, 101 (2): 131–8.

Papadopoulou, T. (2005). Heracles *and Euripidean Tragedy*. Cambridge: Cambridge University Press.

Parke, H. W. (1977). *Festivals of the Athenians*. London: Thames & Hudson.

Parker, R. (1987). 'Myths of Early Athens'. In *Interpretations of Greek Mythology*, ed. J. Bremmer, 187–214. London: Routledge.

Parker, R. (1996). *Athenian Religion: A History*. Oxford: Clarendon Press.

Parker, R. (2009). 'Aeschylus' Gods: Drama, Cult, Theology'. In *Eschyle à l'aube du théâtre occidental: Neuf exposés suivis de discussions: Vandoeuvres–Genève, 25–29 août 2008. Entretiens sur l'Antiquité classique*, ed. J. Jouanna and F. Montanari, chapter 55. Genève: Hardt.

Parry, H. (1965). 'The Second Stasimon of Euripides' Heracles (637–700)'. *American Journal of Philology*, 86 (4): 363–74.

Patterson, L. (2010). *Kinship Myth in Ancient Greece*. 1st edn. Austin, TX: University of Texas Press.

Pickard-Cambridge, A., suppl. J. Gould and D. M. Lewis ([1968] 1988). *The Dramatic Festivals of Athens*. 2nd edn. Oxford: Oxford University Press.

Proietti, G. (2015). 'Beyond the "Invention of Athens": The 5th-Century Athenian "Tatenkatalog" as Example of Intentional History'. *Klio*, 97 (2): 516–38.

Raaflaub, K. A. (1998). 'The Transformation of Athens in the Fifth Century'. In *Democracy, Empire, and the Arts in Fifth-Century Athens*, ed. D. Boedeker and K. A. Raaflaub, 15–42. Cambridge, MA: Harvard Uiversity Press.

Rehm, R. (2002). *The Play of Space: Spatial Transformation in Greek Tragedy*. Princeton, NJ: Princeton University Press.

Rhodes, P. J. (2010). *A History of the Classical World: 478–323*. 2nd edn. Oxford and Malden, MA: Wiley-Blackwell.

Robinson, E. (2008). *Ancient Greek Democracy: Readings and Sources*. Interpreting Ancient History. Oxford: Blackwell.

Rowe, C., and M. Schofield (2000). *The Cambridge History of Greek and Roman Political Thought*. Cambridge: Cambridge University Press.

Rozokoki, A. (2009). 'Some New Thoughts on Stesichorus' Geryoneis'. *Zeitschrift Fur Papyrologie Und Epigraphik*, 168: 3–18.

Rutishauser, B. (2012). *Athens and the Cyclades: Economic Strategies 540–314 BC*. Oxford: Oxford University Press.

Said, S. (1993). 'Tragic Argos'. In *Tragedy, Comedy and the Polis*, Papers from the Greek Drama Conference, Nottingham, 18–20 July 1990, ed. F. S. Halliwell, A. Sommerstein, J. Henderson and B. Zimmermann, 167–89. Bari: Levante Editori.

Sakurai, M., and A. Raubitschek (1987). The Eleusinian Spondai (IG I3 6, lines 8–47). Φιλια επη εις Γεώργιον Ε. Μυλωνάν Β, 263–5. Αθήναι: Η εν Αθήναις Αρχαιολογικής Εταιρείας.

Samons, L. J. (1999). 'Aeschylus, the Alkmeonids and the Reform of the Areopagos'. *Classical Journal*, 94 (3): 221–33.

Samons II, L. J. (2007). 'Conclusion: Pericles and Athens'. In *The Cambridge Companion to the Age of Pericles*, ed. L. J. Samons II, 282–308. Cambridge: Cambridge University Press.

Schmitz, T. A. (2007). *Modern Literary Theory and Ancient Texts: An Introduction*. Oxford: Wiley-Blackwell.

Schultz, P. (2003). 'The Stoa Poikile, the Nike Temple Bastion and Cleon's Shields from Pylos: A Note on Knights 843–859'. *Numismatica e Antichità Classiche*, 32: 43–62.

Scott, M. (2010). *Delphi and Olympia: The Spatial Politics of Panhellenism in the Archaic and Classical Periods*. Cambridge: Cambridge University Press.

Shapiro, H. (1984). 'Herakles and Kyknos'. *American Journal of Archaeology*, 88 (4): 523–9.

Shapiro, H. A. (1989). *Art and Cult under the Tyrants in Athens*. Mainz am Rhein: Philipp Von Zabern.

Shear, Jr, T. (1984). 'The Athenian Agora: Excavations of 1980–1982'. *Hesperia*, 53 (1): 1–57.

Shear, J. L. (2011). *Polis and Revolution: Responding to Oligarchy in Classical Athens*. Cambridge: Cambridge University Press.

Sheppard, J. T. (1916). 'The Formal Beauty of the Hercules Furens'. *Classical Quarterly*, 10: 72–9.

Silk, M. S. (1985). 'Heracles and Greek Tragedy'. *Greece & Rome*, Second Series, 32 (1): 1–22.

Sinn, U. (1993). 'Greek Sanctuaries as Places of Refuge'. In *Greek Sanctuaries: New Approaches*, ed. R. Hagg and N. Marinatos, 70–88. New York: Routledge.

Sinos, R. (1998). 'Divine Selection: Epiphany and Politics in Ancient Greece'. *Cultural Poetics in Archaic Greece*, ed. C. Dougherty and L. Kurke, 73–91. New York and Oxford: Oxford University Press.

Sokolowski, F. (1955). *Lois Sacrées de l'Asie Mineure*. Paris: E. de Boccard.

Sordi, M. (1974). *Contributi dell'Istituto Di Storia Antica*. Vol. 2: *Propaganda e Persuasione Occulta Nell'antichità*. Milano: Vita e pensiero.

Sordi, M. (1975). *Storiografia e Propaganda*. Milano: Università Cattolica del Sacro Cuore.

Sordi, M. (1976). *I Canali Della Propaganda Nel Mondo Antico*. Contributi dell'Istituto di storia antic,a Vol. 4. Milano: Vita e pensiero.

Sourvinou-Inwood, C. (2000). 'What is *Polis* Religion?'. In *Oxford Readings in Greek Religion*, ed. R. Buxton, 13–37. Oxford: Oxford University Press.

Stafford, E. (2012). *Herakles. Gods and Heroes of the Ancient World*. London and New York: Routledge.

Stansbury-O'Donnell, M. (2005). 'The Painting Program in the Stoa Poikile'. In *Periklean Athens and Its Legacy: Problems and Perspectives*, ed. J. M. Barringer and J. M. Hurwit and J. J. Pollitt, 73–87. Austin, TX: University of Texas Press.

Swift, L. A (2010). *The Hidden Chorus: Echoes of Genre in Tragic Lyric*. Oxford: Oxford University Press.

Syme, R. (1939). *The Roman Revolution*. Vol. 1. Oxford: Oxford University Press.

Taplin, O. (1977). *The Stagecraft of Aeschylus: The Dramatic Use of Exits and Entrances in Greek Tragedy*. Oxford: Clarendon Press.

Taplin, O. (2007). *Pots & Plays: Interactions Between Tragedy and Greek Vase-Painting of the Fourth Century B.C.* Los Angeles, CA: J. Paul Getty Museum.

Taylor, J. G. (1998). 'Oinoe and the Painted Stoa: Ancient and Modern Misunderstandings?'. *American Journal of Philology*, 119 (2): 223–43.

Taylor, M. (1991). *The Tyrant Slayers: The Heroic Image in Fifth Century B.C. Athenian Art and Politics*. 2nd edn. Salem, NH: Ayer Co. Publishers.

Thomas, R. (1989). *Oral Tradition & Written Records in Classical Athens*. Cambridge: Cambridge University Press.

Thompson, G. F. (2003). 'Approaches to "Performance": An Analysis of Terms'. *Performance: Critical Concepts in Literary and Cultural Studies*, ed. P. Auslander, 138–52. London: Routledge.

Thompson, H. A. (1962). 'The Sculptural Adornment of the Hephaisteion'. *American Journal of Archaeology*, 66 (3): 339–47.

Trendall, A. D., and T. Webster (1971). *Illustrations of Greek Drama*. London: Phaidon.

Turner, M. (2006). *The Artful Mind: Cognitive Science and the Riddle of Human Creativity*. Oxford: Oxford University Press.

Tzanetou, A. (2012). *City of Suppliants: Tragedy and the Athenian Empire*. Austin, TX: University of Texas Press.

Verbank-Piérard, A. (1992). 'Heracles at Feast in Attic Art: A Mythical or Cultic Iconography'. In *The Iconography of Greek Cult in the Archaic and Classical Periods*, ed. R. Hägg, 85–106. Liège: Presse universitaires de Liège.

Vilariño Rodriguez, J. J. (2010). 'La Evolución del Arquero en el Contexto Bélico Griego'. *El Futuro Del Pasado*, 1: 263–77.

Von den Hoff, R. (2009). 'Herakles, Theseus and the Athenian Treasury at Delphi'. In *Structure, Image, Ornament: Architectural Sculpture in the Greek World*, Proceedings of an International Conference held at the American School of Classical Studies, 27–28 November 2004, ed. P. Schultz and R. von den Hoff, 96–104. Oxford and Oakville, CT: Oxbow Books.

Walker, H. (1995). *Theseus and Athens*. New York and Oxford: Oxford University Press.

Wilamowitz-Moellendorff, U. von (1889). *Euripides: Herakles*. Berlin: Weidmannsche Buchhandlung.

Wilson, P. (2000). *The Athenian Institution of the Khoregia: The Chorus, the City, and the Stage*. Cambridge: Cambridge University Press.

Wilson, P. (1997). 'Leading the Tragic Khoros: Tragic Prestige in the Democratic City'. In *Greek Tragedy and the Historian*, ed. C. Pelling, 81–108. Oxford: Clarendon Press.

Winkler, J. J. (1992). *Nothing to do with Dionysos? Athenian Drama in Its Social Context*. Princeton, NJ: Princeton University Press.

Winnington-Ingram, R. P. (1980). *Sophocles: an Interpretation*. Cambridge: Cambridge University Press.

Woodford, S. (1966). 'Exemplum Virtutis: A Study of Heracles in Athens in the Second Half of the Fifth Century BC'. PhD diss., Columbia University.

Woolf, G. D. (1997). 'Polis-Religion and Its Alternatives in the Roman Provinces'. In *Römische Reichsreligion Und Provinzialreligion*, ed. H. Cancik and J. Rüpke, 71–84. Tübingen: Mohr Siebeck.

Yates, D. C. (2019). *States of Memory: The Polis, Panhellenism, and the Persian War*. Oxford: Oxford University Press.

Yunis, H. (1988). *A New Creed: Fundamental Religious Beliefs in the Athenian Polis and Euripidean Drama*. Göttingen Vandenhoeck & Ruprecht.

Zanker, P. (1990). *The Power of Images in the Age of Augustus (Thomas Spencer Jerome Lectures)*. Ann Arbor, MI: University of Michigan Press.

Zeitlin, F. (1990). 'Thebes: Theater of Self and Society in Athenian Drama'. In *Nothing to Do with Dionysos? Athenian Drama in Its Social Context*, ed. J. J. Winkler and F. I. Zeitlin, 130–67. Princeton, NJ: Princeton University Press.

Ziolkowski, J. (1981). *Thucydides and the Tradition of Funeral Speeches at Athens*. New York: Ayer.

Zuntz, G. (1955). *The Political Plays of Euripides*. Manchester: Manchester University Press.

Index

Acropolis 16, 26, 28, 30, 31, 42, 44, 46, 67, 71, 79, 102
   Peisistratean Acropolis 61, 79
Aeschylus 125
   Oresteia 106–7, 107–11
      Agamemnon 114
         121: 114
      Eumenides 103, 110, 114, 116, 143 n.12
   Prometheus Unbound 56
Agamemnon 82, 84–5, 96
   play, *see under* Aeschylus
Agora (Athenian) 27, 31, 67, 70–80
Ajax 34, 95–7
   play, *see under* Sophocles
Ajax minor 75, 77
   play, *see under* Sophocles *Ajax Locrus*
Akamas and Demophon 75–6
Alcmaeonidai 18, 36, 65–6
Amphitryon 3, 83, 90–1, 95–6, 106, 109, 112, 114, 115, 118
Apollo 20
   Delos 37, 123
   Delphi 18, 36, 63, 64–6, 69
   Heracles 99, 110
Apollodorus
   Bibliotheca
      2.4.48–9: 100
aristocracy (aristocratic values) *see also* εὐγενία
   and Athenian democracy 10, 25, 32–6, 61, 65–7, 96, 127
   definition 33–4, 89–90
   and Heracles 3, 69, 77, 89, 91–2, 94, 95–7, 112, 115, 119, 124, 126, 128
Aristogeiton, *see* Harmodius and Aristogeiton
Aristophanes
   Acharnians
      502–4: 15

Birds 56–7
Frogs 56–7
Plutus 845 (scholia on) 50
Aristotle
   [*Athenaion Politeia*]
      19.4: 18
      54.7: 136 n.26
   Rhetorica ii.22.1396a: 125
ἀρχή, *see under* Delian League
Athena 26, 30–1, 49, 54, 55, 56, 63–4, 105
   and *Heracles* 87, 94, 102–3, 107–11, 119, 122
   iconography 44, 46, 51, 66, 69, 75–6, 78
   and Peisistratus 20–2, 29, 42–3
audience
   and Attic drama 14, 29, 58
   and cultural surface 2, 6, 7–8, 9–10, 41, 59
   and iconography 61, 73, 80
   original reception of the play 3, 85, 94, 97, 100, 102–3, 104, 107, 109, 110, 118, 120–1
   and propaganda 22–3, 127, 128
autochthony 26, 30–6, 113, 116–17

Barbarians 21, 72, 74–7, 126
bow (Heracles') 54, 87, 91, 117

Cecrops 26–7, 30
chorus 29, 87, 93–5, 96, 100, 107, 108, 109, 111–16, 122
Cimon 20, 69, 70–2, 73, 76, 79–80
communication 4, 7, 23–4, 26, 46, 62, 109
Creophylus of Samos
   Sack of Oichalia 138 n.52
cultural surface 9–10, 13, 43, 46, 59, 69, 121, 127–8
   definition 6–8

Delian League 10, 14, 53, 58
   ἀρχή 15, 26, 36–9, 75, 122, 123 125–6

Delphi 51, 52, 75, 128
   and Alcmaeonidai 18, 36
   Athenian Treasury 62–70, 79, 80, 97
   and *Heracles* 99–100, 110, 124
δίκη, *see* justice

education 23, 27, 35–6, 114
Eleusis 31, 45–6, 50–3, 100, 120, 127
epic, *see* Homer
Erechtheus 26–7
εὐγενία 89–92, 113, 119
Euripides
   Alcestis 56–7, 90
   Auge 56–7
   Erechthonius 16
   Eurystheus 57
   Heracles
      4–8: 116
      26–43: 108
      53–9: 93
      84–5: 93
      91: 95
      105–6: 95
      110–11: 111
      144: 95
      168–9: 108
      190: 91
      198: 91
      225–6: 83
      220: 91
      227–35: 93
      295–7: 95
      303–5: 93
      308: 90
      339: 93
      343: 109
      348: 114
      454: 91
      460–1: 95
      467–85: 117
      505–6: 95
      520–2: 93
      551: 93
      568–73 (572): 84, 88
      582: 83
      613: 120
      765: 100
      780ff: 144 n.26
      798–801: 109
      814: 112
      838–42: 89, 101–2, 104, 106
      843–63: 86
      851–2: 82, 91
      855–7: 101–2
      931–4: 84
      935–40: 86–7
      971: 88
      989: 87
      992: 87
      1001–8: 102
      1153–4: 94
      1163–71: 116
      1165: 94
      1220ff: 94
      1225: 94
      1227–8: 90
      1234: 108
      1243: 108, 120
      1248: 120
      1252: 83
      1253: 120
      1262–4: 109
      1322–35 (1323–35): 91, 102
      1331–5: 115, 120
      1340–6: 103–4, 105
      1350: 91
      1357: 91
      1375: 91
      1382: 91
      1383: 83
      1388: 91
      1403: 91, 94
      1425–6: 95
      1427–8: 115
   Heraclidae 2, 57, 116, 117
      847–66: 57
   Hippolytus 2, 57, 139 n.61, 144 n.23
   Ion 9, 16, 31, 65
   Orestes 100, 142 n.18
   Peirithous 57
   Supplices. 2, 16, 107, 116, 117
      428–62: 32
   Trojan Women 9
Eurystheus 3, 48, 86–8, 117
   play, *see under* Euripides

friendship 2–3, 35, 91, 92–5, 96, 112, 115, 112, 124

funeral oration 113–15, 122
    Pericles 32, 107, 113

Great Dionysia 13–15, 37, 128

Harmodius and Aristogeiton 21–2, 27–8, 70
Hera 85–6, 99, 100–6, 109–10
Heraclidae 28, 32, 49, 124, 125
    play, *see under* Euripides
Herodotus 20–1, 29, 43, 76
    1.60.3–5: 20–1
    1. 66–8: 20, 131 n.14
    5. 62.3: 18
    8.144.2: 19
Hesiod 55–6
    [*Shield*] 55 138 n.52
    Theogonia
        523–31: 55
        316–18: 56
Hipparchus 22, 27
Hippias 27, 36
Hippolytus 100
    play, *see under* Euripides
Homer 14, 75, 87–8, 107, 125
    Heracles in 54–6
    Homeric gods 103, 104, 105
    Homeric heroes 26, 76, 82, 83–5, 96, 97, 102, 104
    Homeric hymns 54, 138 n.51
    Homeric values 34–5, 64–5, 83–5, 87–8, 96, 105
    Iliad
        5.403–4: 54
        6.467–71: 88
        8.299: 84
        8.362–9: 55, 56
        9.239: 84
        9.305: 84
        13.52: 84
        15.607: 141 n.5
        16.431–61: 101–2
        21.542: 84
        15.605–12: 84
        18.334–5: 84
        19.85–138: 84–5
        20.145–7: 56
        23.20–1: 84
        23.182–3: 84

Odyssey
    8.223–5: 54
    11.626: 55, 56

Inscriptiones Graecae
    IG I^2 22: 132 n.36
    IG I^2 39: 132 n.36
    IG I^2 71: 134 n.52
    IG I^3 6: 53
    IG I^3 10: 132 n.36
    IG I^3 78: 52
    IG II^2 1933: 137 n.39
Ion 23, 32, 37–8, 53, 125–7
    play, *see under* Euripides
Isocrates
    Panegyricus
        28–9: 138 n.48
        63: 144 n.24

justice 13
    Athens 31, 75, 76–7, 125, 126
    Heracles 86, 99, 100–2, 106–11, 115

khoregia 14, 29, 32, 64, 96

labours 51, 54, 55
    in *Heracles* 3, 58, 82–3, 85, 86, 87, 89, 93, 94, 96, 99–100, 110, 113–14, 117, 124
    in iconography 44–7, 66–9, 78, 113–14
Leithourgia, *see khoregia*
Lycus 3, 86, 89–91, 95, 100–1, 107, 108–11, 114, 118

Megara 87–8, 93, 95, 102, 112, 117, 118
Miltiades 20, 65, 68–9, 71, 79

Oeta (Mt) 3, 58
Olympia 46, 51, 52, 65, 78, 102, 113–14
    Olympic games 41, 55, 123
Olympus 43–5, 46, 81
Orestes 31, 62, 100, 107, 108, 110, 142 n.1
    bones of 20, 131 n.16
    play, *see under* Euripides

Pausanias 72–4, 77
    1.15.1–3: 73, 136 n.28
    1.17.2–3: 140 n.30
    1.19.3: 47

1.32.4: 136 n.28
10.10.1: 140 n.21
Peisistratus 2, 20–2, 29, 42–4, 50
performance
　of Athenian drama 1, 5, 6, 13–15
　Homeric poems 34
　theory 6–7
Pindar 54–6
　Isthmian
　　iv.11–12: 136 n.20
　Nemean
　　i.61–3: 138 n.55
　　iii.22: 47, 55
　　x.32–3: 55
　　xi.27–8: 55
　Olympian
　　i.5–7: 55
　　i. 60–72: 55
　　ii.2–4: 55
　　iii.11–35: 55
　　vi.67–8: 55
　　x.20–30: 55, 138 n.55
Pisander of Rhodes
　Heracleia 138 n.52
Plato 17, 30
　Politicus
　　290 c–d: 17
　Laws
　　909d–910a: 17
　Republic
　　414 d–e: 30, 132 n.28
Plutarch
　Apophthegmata Laconica 236b–c
　　133 n.38
　Vitae
　　Alcibiades
　　　11: 145 n.1
　　Cimon
　　　7.3–8.1: 71
　　Nicias
　　　3: 145 n.1
　　Themistocles
　　　1.2: 47
　　Theseus
　　　36.2: 20
pottery
　Athens, NM 401 135 n.6
　Heidelberg P, Berlin (West), Staatl.
　　Mus. V. I. 3151 136 n.10

Heracles in 2, 42–6, 49, 56, 57, 102,
　127
Madrid, Arch. Mus. 10915 136 n.10
MuM Sonderliste R (1977) no. 22
　136 n.10
Naples, Mus.Naz. 8117 135 n.6
New York 17.230.14 135 n.6
Paris, Louvre CA 598 136 n.10
and politics 7, 31, 42–3
Reggio Calabria Museo Naz. 4001
　51

reception
　modern 1, 6, 16
　theory of 4–5
　see also under audience: *Original
　　reception of the play*

Sophocles
　Ajax 95–7, 126
　　330: 142 n.20
　　349: 142 n.20
　　477–8: 95
　　481–526: 34
　　587–8: 34
　　900–14: 34
　　1381: 95
　Ajax Locrus 75
　Athamas 56
　Heracles in 56–9
　Oedipus Coloneus 116, 117
　Oedipus Tyrannus 4
　Philoctetes 57
　Trachiniae 57–8
Sparta
　and the Alcmaeonidai / overthrow of
　　Athenian tyranny 18, 27–8,
　　36
　and Athens 31, 52, 73–4, 100, 110,
　　126–7
　and bones of Orestes, *see* Orestes
　and Heracles 41, 49, 124, 123
　and the Leagues 36, 125, 126–7
　Spartan ideology 2, 41
Stesichorus 138 n.52
suppliants 16, 17, 87–8, 96–7, 101, 106–7,
　109, 118–19
　for the play by Euripides, *see Supplices*
　　under Euripides

thesauroi 32–3, 63
   Athenian at Delphi 62–70
Theseus 26, 31, 42, 57, 58–9, 107, 117, 125
   cult 48–50
   bones of 20, 71–2
   iconography 44–6, 52–3, 61, 65–9, 74,
         78–80, 97, 105, 108, 112, 115,
         119–20, 121–2, 124
   in the play 83, 91–2, 93–4, 95, 97, 102–3
   sons of, *see* Akamas and Demophon
Thucydides 29, 123, 125
   1.20: 27–8
   1.44: 134 n.52
   1.77: 132–3 n.36
   2.37.1: 32
   2.41.4: 125
   2.42.1: 113
   52.9–14 : 51
Triptolemos 31, 51–3

vases, *see* pottery

Xenophon
   Hellenica 6.3.6: 52
   Memorabilia ii 1.21–34: 135 n.9

Zeus 46, 65, 81, 82, 89–90, 93, 100–3, 105,
         106, 109–10, 118, 122

www.ingramcontent.com/pod-product-compliance
Lightning Source LLC
Chambersburg PA
CBHW052126300426
44116CB00010B/1807